SUKUN

ALSO BY KAZIM ALI

WESLEYAN POETRY

O

SUKUN

Kazim Ali

NEW AND SELECTED

POEMS

O

Wesleyan University Press   Middletown, Connecticut

Wesleyan University Press
Middletown CT 06459
www.wesleyan.edu/wespress

Manufactured in the United States of America
Designed and typeset in Whitman by Eric M. Brooks

Library of Congress Cataloging-in-Publication Data
Names: Ali, Kazim, 1971– author.
Title: Sukun : new and selected poems / Kazim Ali.
Other titles: Sukun (Compilation)
Description: Middletown, Connecticut : Wesleyan University Press, [2023] |
    Series: Wesleyan poetry | Summary: "A selection of verse and prose poems
    published in earlier books along with previously unpublished new poems" —
    Provided by publisher.
Identifiers: LCCN 2023001754 (print) | LCCN 2023001755 (ebook) |
    ISBN 9780819500700 (cloth) | ISBN 9780819500717 (trade paperback) |
    ISBN 9780819500724 (ebook)
Subjects: BISAC: POETRY / LGBTQ+ | POETRY / Canadian | LCGFT: Poetry.
Classification: LCC PS3601.L375 S85 2023 (print) | LCC PS3601.L375 (ebook) |
    DDC 811/.6—dc23/eng/20230425
LC record available at https://lccn.loc.gov/2023001754
LC ebook record available at https://lccn.loc.gov/2023001755

5 4 3 2 1

TO JEAN VALENTINE

after late music a rest

CONTENTS

o

TERNARY

o

PRAYER FOR CHASM

What you ask for
Hold me whole
New moon wants you
Unseen   unctuous
Willing to go to any length
To rise

You lie on your back
In cold spring lost
Or tossed
How they are the same
Both questions to a world
Unanswerable

You were never known
None can spell your name
So impossible you un-
Pronounce never in
Knowable days able to be
In a place be a person

Who speaks who thinks   .
Who does the laundry
Always instead this dealer
Of done deals of what's
Done after dun plain
Grass wanting then to lie

At the beach sun and sky
And salt let it all have
You have at you
Jailed at the shore sure

That the near star will un-
Ravel solar threads to spin

In gold squares a new
Narrative of normal the one
Where you stop answering
The one where you stop
Asking how deep this hole
The chasm between

Who you were are thought
You would be you do not
Cross are not afraid
The chasm is a thought
Who is thinking
I will live

GOLDEN BOY

Almost afraid I am in the annals of history to speak
       And by speaking be seen by man or god
             Such then debt in light be paid

Atop the Manitoban parliament building in Winnipeg
       What beacon to dollars food or god shine
          I hallow starvation

This nation a notion beneath the body hollowing
       Its stomach to emptiness and in breadth
          The river empties

Who sew spoke the craft born along
       Long echo and echelon grains of light
          And space we width one and other weight

The soul not the spirit breathe through
       Spirited went or wend why true
          Weave woe we've woven

A dozen attempts these tents pitched
       On the depth be made biped by pen may
          Perch atop the temple pool

Proven now prove these riches of wheat and
       Cherries and prunes what washes
          Over woven ocean

Frayed I am most sir desired
       Sired in wind seared and warned
          Once in wild umiyak sworn

We parley to mend be conned be bent
        Come now called to document your
                Meant intent your indented mind

Haul oh star your weight in aeons
        There in prayer money morrow more
                You owe and over time god spends

The spent river melt into
        Summer sound out the window
                Sound out the spender

Where does the river road end
        In what language can prayer or
                Commerce be offered

Ender of senses pensive atop
        Plural spires be spoken or mended
                Broken and meant for splendor my mentor

EXIT STRATEGY

I hear the sound of the sprinkler outside,
not the soft kind we used to run through
but the hard kind that whips in one direction
then cranks back and starts again.

Last night we planned to find the white argument
of the Milky Way but we are twenty years too late.

Last night I cut the last stargazer
lily to wear in my hair.

Here's the hardest geography quiz I've ever taken:
How does one carry oneself from mountain to lake to desert
without leaving anything behind?

Perhaps I ought to have worked harder. Perhaps I could have
paid more attention. A mountain I didn't climb. Music I yearned for
but could not achieve.

I travel without maps, free-style my scripture,
pretend the sky is an adequate representation
of my spiritual beliefs.

The sprinkler switches off. The grass will be wet.
I haven't even gotten to page 2 of my life and
I'm probably more than halfway through,
who knows what kind of creature I will become.

o

FROM

THE FAR

MOSQUE

o

GALLERY

You came to the desert, illiterate, spirit-ridden,
intending to starve

The sun hand of the violin carving through space
the endless landscape

Acres of ochre, the dust-blue sky,
or the strange young man beside you

peering into "The Man Who Taught William Blake
Painting in His Dreams"

You are thinking: *I am ready to be touched now, ready to be found*
He is thinking: *How lost, how endless I feel this afternoon*

When will you know:
all night: sounds

Violet's brief engines
The violin's empty stomach resonates

Music a scar unraveling in four strings
An army of hungry notes shivers down

You came to the desert intending to starve   so starve

RENUNCIATION

The Sailor cannot see the North —
but knows the Needle can —

The books were all torn apart, sliced along the spines
Light filled all the openings that she in her silence renounced

Still: her handwriting on the papers remembered us to her
The careful matching of the papers' edges was a road back

One night Muhammad was borne aloft by a winged horse
Taken from the Near Mosque to the Far Mosque

Each book likens itself to lichen,
stitching softly to tree trunks, to rocks

what was given into the Prophet's ears that night:
A changing of directions — now all the scattered tribes must pray:

Wonder well foundry, well sunborn, sundered and sound here
Well you be found here, foundered and found

THE AGNES MARTIN ROOM

What is a question to someone who practices years of silence?

Stones skim the water's surface, shimmer there, lost.

In the window sound of last year.

Swim dimmer there.

After four days without speaking, I don't ask questions anymore.

Given a line, drawn through space.

Reach to reason to region.   To seem or sum
Sun or stone.

Could weep here.

Sleep here.

In the sweep of watery gray.

On white, the wishes, the whispered accounts,
a little autobiography, littered on the surface.

Where we listen. Were we here.

Unaccountable dark matter of the universe,
an utterly supportless planet. Ocean of space.

All the same river to read. All shapes or landscape.

The scapegoat silent, following the road of devotion.

Going down without air.

Sounds like the rope against the side of the boat, a hollow bell.

Getting subtler and subtler in the acres of water until
one refuses to return.

Spirit send the question sound.

Painting is the quicksand back.

Two tracks over the seeming field of white.

All the eventual answers are nothing.

Painting is asking you.

No time is passing.

SOURCE

In the brain, a silver window
Where the sky evaporates—

Then condenses to an enveloped name
Sealed with an unsigned letter.

Dickinson's house: a breeze coming from the inside
Sounds bury themselves deep in the wood-work.

When a Scholar pauses by a closed door
She may not be listening to music, but to the door

What lingers in the letter, loosening or found
Sky-name—wood-wind—syllable—sound

SPEECH

How struck I was by that face, years ago, in the church mural:
Eve, being led by Christ through the broken gates of Hell.

She's been nominated for the position of Featured Saint
on the Icon of Belief, up against the dark horse candidate—

Me: fever-ridden and delirious, a child in Vellore, unfolding
the packet around my neck that I was ordered not to open.

Inside, a folk cure, painted delicately in saffron.
Letters that I could not read.

Why I feel qualified for the position
based on letters I could not read amounts to this:

Neither you nor I can pronounce the difference
between the broken gates and the forbidden letters.

So what reason do we need to believe in icons or saints?
How might we otherwise remember—

without an image to fasten in that lonely place—
the rock on which a Prophet flung himself into fever?

Without icon or church, spell "gates of Hell."
Spell "those years ago unfolding."

Recite to me please all the letters you are not able to read.
Spell "fling yourself skyward."

Spell "fever."

AGNES MARTIN

Wetten to work here seen against the sky sandscape sandbox silent

Alone mind unleashed mouth a close open cave stone breathe

Stone whiten away sharp sky edge dusk blend down dark self edge

Thrown aloft five birds little surface wind lettered and fettered

Distant sounds littered across thoughts sounds blanked pulled taut

Spun thunder then well spread encumbered better window bitter

Sun wind whispered winter went indigo wild wick lit wend home

Sleep-written swept sweetly remind here my mend here my mind

Hear sweep music slides fabric oceanic oh shine year light shine

Year come time ear tie signs and sing why think river open heart I

Cornflower cowslip field wind settled across year sound thrown

Settled to end hear whittled to wend—

TRAVEL

Soon to leave

Soon across the water

Prepare the white clothes

I will not plan the painting

But travel—the trees—

Looking out over the roofs

Rather lay paint directly on the canvas

Kate writes from Paris, in smoke

I can't respond but pack

The painting is not finished until the original idea has been

Taken down from the walls

All the paintings

Enough nomad, move through "soon"

Move through

Obliterated

DEPARTURE

My last evening spent wandering along the docks.
By the foot-path, great iron rings.

Here is where the boats moor when the water rises.

The clouds gather themselves tightly together
as dervishes do after a period of whirling.

This should be a black and white film,
where I am the only one left,

sitting in front of the café,
waiting for the rain.

Briefly the sun pierces the clouds,
casts eerie shadows.

The waiter's shirt glows white.
My little cup glows white.

Letters in my bag for mailing.
Starlings clamber on the depot roof.

The sun dips into late afternoon.
For ten years I could not see.

Two boys are stacking rocks on top of one another.
I close my eyes and listen to the falling.

What about yesterday and the day before that?
Carry what you can in your hands. Scatter the rest.

TRAIN RIDE

We take a compartment. I draw the curtains and shut the door so that other passengers will believe the seats are all filled and leave us.

This rudeness is against my cousin's instincts, so I let him take the backwards facing seat.

He says it is the proper way to view the landscape.

That night in Aix-en-Provence we won't be able to find a hotel, and the hostel will be closed.

We will spend all night in the public square, reciting poetry to one another, and receiving gifts from late-night locals.

Flowers, drawings, hot pastries.

This moment now gone.

I time everything to that current of lapse.

No absent time.

Even in deep space, there are particles of dark matter that do not add matter to the mass of the universe.

Versions of the story wither over sacred fire. A prophet's willingness to be blind.

We travel alone all the way to Marseille. Or: while my cousin uses the bathroom, two girls come to sit with me.

We have to switch trains at Dijon. Or: we never make it as far as Aix.

The source of a vision only a priestess getting high on fumes.

Snake-licked. Shucking off the old skin.

Blessed be the undone version. The train actually stalls on the tracks for several hours, during which we contemplate returning to Paris.

It might only be a condition of the window glass that allows me to see the subtle ridges and gradations in the clouds, the swirling depth of the sky.

A Cézanne painting on the cover of *The World of the Ten Thousand Things* is so deathly unfinished it looks nearly transparent. Pencil marks on the canvas.

Later, in a vestibule between cars, the Provençal sun setting, I catch sight of the book's cover in the reflection of the window.

Flooded with bright orange and yellow the painting completes itself.

Is that all: a quest for fulfillment satisfied by the correct conditions? In this case, supposed chromatic equations of the southern skies—my cousin explains it: yellow in Arles, green in Aix, purple on the Côte d'Azur.

Later he will return to Paris, and I will hike alone to Saintes-Maries-de-la-Mer where Magdalen supposedly washed ashore with her servant Sarah. Their bones are in a reliquary in the church.

Yet another church miles and miles to the north and east of here continues the story: Magdalen left her servant and traveled inland with the Romani and died there.

Another set of bones in that church.

Unlike in mathematics, every quadratic equation in history does not necessarily have an equivalent modular form.

Small handfuls only create an *impression* of a manageable amount to hold. For example, I have left out the wild flamingos, a subtle swipe of pale pink along their pearl-white bodies, flying across the road; also the horse-back ride through the swamps of the Cammargue, the hours I sat in the small shack in the bird sanctuary, the black-clad Romani woman I saw in the market.

In the tarot book, past and future shuffle and re-shuffle.

As our journey progresses we do eventually open the curtains and the compartment fills.

We eat the previously unmentioned camembert sandwiches.

We won't arrive in Aix for several more hours and don't go on to Cassis for four more days after that.

Where, in another four days, in the mountains above the city, tired and out of money and ready to go home, we will meet Mister Stevarius, the Belgian Fire Eater, and everything changes.

THE YEAR OF SUMMER

You came down from the mountains to the shore with your father's voice ringing in your ears, saying over and over again the call to prayer.

The stairs leading down to the water are cracked and marked by awakening.

Awakening in the south the morning sun shines lemon yellow for eleven months, the leaves of the trees telling a book of eleven dreams.

In this book, the sky is sometimes lavender. In this book are colors you have never seen before.

In this book is the taste of white peach.

The blue-black sea turns milky under the noon sun.

In the twelfth dream your father whispers your name into each of your folded ears.

In the year of summer you came south into a city of yellow and white, and what was told of this city was told in trees, and then in leaves, and then in light.

NIGHT BOAT

At some point in the calanques above Cassis
You were told by Mister Stevarius the Belgian Fire Eater

Falling down the mountain the lights of the night boat to Corsica
Disappear the rock of Cassis, thrust out into the sea

That there would be a moment at which

The road to the temple of the sun threads its secret way
From the violent tongue of the third calanque to the rocky alcove

Where the cliff-climbers muscle their way up, unsupported

You would no longer hear

Everyone is talking loud
The schoolteacher from Aix is drunk

and the accountant from Switzerland
calls the German a bastard for not sharing his coffee

There you are on the night boat, hungry
Fire on the surface of the water

Letters collecting in the groundswell
You will not hour

On the beach of sound, waves roam back to open sea
Close to the surface the sun's setting pools orange

An opening of light in the sky
A stripe of rubble you've never seen before

Unfurl your hands to say:
The trees are rapt with silence

The burning bird settling in the rocks
Stand ever among the broken vowels:

You will no longer here

The silent groundswell, the swell of silence.

RAIN

With thick strokes of ink the sky fills with rain.
Pretending to run for cover, secretly I pray for more rain.

Over the echo of the water, I hear a voice saying my name.
No one in the city moves under the quick sightless rain.

The pages of my notebook soak, then curl. I've written:
"Yogis opened their mouths for hours to drink the rain."

The sky is a bowl of dark water, rinsing your face.
The window trembles; liquid glass could shatter into rain.

I am a dark bowl, waiting to be filled.
If I open my mouth now, I could drown in the rain.

I hurry home as though someone is there waiting for me.
The night collapses into your skin. I am the rain.

THICKET

The story unfolds like this: A blameless father
loves the as yet unharmed son.

The son is somewhat randy and alarmed
at his appearance in an orthodox world.

Does it hurt him that he's been cut from the tribe of sons
who believe, are unarmed, who recite all the rules?

It's the father that believes in God.
The son believes in his father.

The father in this story is guileless,
not trying to call God's bluff.

And unbelievably to all,
the son willingly opens his throat to the universe.

Neither one of them seeking to see God,
They are not saying His name, not asking to be saved.

THE RETURN OF MUSIC

The bridge of birches stretches down to the horizon.
A ridge of wings descending into the leaves.

Turn now in a note sent thither.
Thither around and the wind strikes.

Orange, the trees are aflame.
Scarlet. Called here, you came.

Light carving shadows into tree bark.
You translate this into other languages, all antiquated and still.

An anthem of ether. Shorn, you always wondered:
what willful course have you carved through your history?

In the tree-capped valley, the lustrous wind chafes through.
Leaf fence uncurl. The valley wends the way the music went.

The sapphire sky, unbelievable, but there.
These moments against the years you cannot believe.

This hover of music winging down from the mountains
you cannot believe.

But here in the trees, here above the river, here as the season
stitches itself into fog then frost, you will.

Here as you unfold, unsummon, uncry, you will.

Unopened, you will. Unhappen, you will.

These moments against the years, you will.

Unmoment you will.

Unyear you will. Unyou you will.

Unwill you will—

DEAR RUMI

You've forgotten the other life in which
Shams-e-Tabriz threw your books into the fountain.

The ink, finally unrecognizable,
reached for you with dissipating lust.

Once I went up the mountain at daybreak, and still met pilgrims
coming down who had woken for the journey earlier.

In the tomb of not-Shams I prayed and prayed to be not-found.
Am I the sun inside me?

Shams will walk out the back door and never return.
You will go mad—spend years looking for him.

One day in the marketplace, estranged and weeping,
you will understand the farthest mosque is the one within,

and that the sun in the sky is not the one you orbit around,
nor the one who went out the back door and never returned.

Somewhere in the world now, every minute,
a sun is dropping over the horizon into yesterday.

At the fountain in the village square,
the books are still sinking, bereft of your hands.

Even the mountains are bending down to try to save them.
Dear Shams-e-Tabriz, I do not mourn.

You spindle me, sun-thorn, to the sky.

MAYA OR MAA'

You will always be gone.
All matter edges itself to dust.

Sunlight a pool or flower or fountain.
Music breaking the room to shards.

But why fret? In one language *maya* means
"all these molecules are breaking."

Your hands, the music, the paper, are not real.
Not pieces of liquid or light, but light years.

On the other side of the world you were taught
other names for things.

Mr. William touches the surface of the water with his hand,
says: *maa'*.

Water, light, light on the surface of the water
or shining from beneath the water, are all fibs and fortunes.

Music can break its fall.
Light could speak.

A year could open between *maya* and *maa'*
that would provide perfect pitch against which you could practice.

Beyond that you're flailing, moon-licked, stunned,
Music, sunstruck, rainstorm, begun—

RHYME

Restless your surface rise up be unraveled
Unwrap the dusk to a light shell

All the crevices in the oak are pierced by moon chords
Rough sky unlocked shredded by meteors

Vision-dusted thirsty night's blue fastenings
Second time this earth year the sun I leapt up in anger

Birch bark unribbons to reveal all the secret roads
Sun soaks the day's façade in clouds and clots

How fully I tack myself to the wind of anger
While you life up the mountain match-struck immaculate

Sun oracle prophesy solar flares along my skin
Wind oracle forgive me perennially rude

A long secret road unfastens from earth
Frozen luck-thin snapping in unseasonable cold

Four white roads crossing nothing into nothing
Such low light through the bottle hanging

Breath sieve mountain come break at the sea
When lava that new country first enters the water

The rock an immense fire river pouring onto the beach
Saying all the words in the world rhyme

Will wind winterful wending flood
A bell brooding somewhere oracle

A wolf-note sounding against the hush
Somewhere thorned to the sun-spindle

Spendthrift wind run spindle din drift
Music kin shift cindered candle theft

Soot riddle wicked fire
Ash answer wind mouth

Cave earth throat explain
Why all the unhinged worlds rhyme

Olga omen old friend
Meddle metal birth foam

Green notebook winter road
Over sound world sheet

Ocean home metal written sun verse
Curt whisper absurd wishes winter thirst

JULY

We lay down in the graveyard, hinged there.

Emerald moss growing thickly in the chiseled letters.

You're explaining how trees actually breathe.

Green in the names and trees went up to join gray in the sky.

Then the gray-green sky came down in breaths to my lips and sipped me.

o

FROM

THE
FORTIETH
DAY

o

LOSTNESS

dear God of blankness I pray to dear unerasable

how could I live without You if I were ever given answers

the summer thickens with lostness

lovers who will not touch each other but look out into space

thinking I do not belong in the world

news always travels inland but how can this storm

be undone or the treacherous rain unravel or the train

arriving one street over and all night long

on an island at the end of islands a foresworn vow

a river blasted through and another river filled in

dear afternoon God dear evening God dear lonely world

the circles of water and wanton violence

dear utterly unmistakable ether

dear Lostness your careless supplicant drops everything

and rakes over me on his way to an implacable place

MORNING PRAYER

the work of dark
a tremulous sound

Mount Beacon season to season
changes or is changed

what's in us that reaches
to know what's after

should I draw the spirit
as a lantern or a cup

DEAR SUNSET, DEAR AVALANCHE

dear thunder without lightning
dear window sound of last year

dear mountainous landscape
unfolding

water in air unraveling
dear ice-filled clamor that fetches

I'm fetching, tolling, a libelous suit
sold and soldiering up the slopes

navigating the trails without adequate supplies
opening up the roof of the ride

a somnambulist, a compassless climber,
a lunchless hack, naked on the rock road

my ear cocked to the distance
dear solo slipping sun

this is the part the slow whispering interrupts
dear disappeared, dear desperate

this is the part you're always interrupting,
the part you want to be buried under—

CAVE

There is a web of blue and green in his dream,
seedlings of sky and grass thrusting up from the ground.

Years after his promise to his body was broken
and the silver cord severed

the spirit sent like a ghost ship to trawl the dream terrain,
wrinkled and blue—

Music leaks roughly from the body
the way the stomach empties itself of vomit—

Days and days after he stays weak
making the promise, writing it into all the crevices and corners—

One vow could cut through all the surf,
commend him to a steady stream of silver cords—

But isn't it better, his tricky innards reason with him,
to be like this: lost, afraid, hungry and alone,

deafened in the cave of your own breath,
no web spun across the mouth, no angel inside—

VASE

He wrote to you once, night's cold I,
storm-broken branches,

here in this room on the galaxy's edge.

He wrote to you twice, sun-yellow dusk,
midnight enameled vase,

snow-blue shelf in the sky.

He wrote to you three times,
and the nothing inside flew up,

a listless prisoner, tethered, a spy

ORNITHOGRAPHY

sunlight alarms the room
tattered by time and the failed window

dust motes taking note of the yellow
as it passes through the glass in bars without breaking

a difficult spill from the blue leading to an idea
the sky is you, the bird was you, the glass was you,

are you still, though all broken—

if you sail out on your boat will the air unroll,
will it open into navigable paths

will you single out the sound that lingers
a bow that shivers along the strings

a transcription of the sight of five hundred wings
dreaming a sudden maze

whose feathered arms are gesturing
through dust's field of vision

when you the boat wake
when the rudder drifts

the surface is still
is it really still since still reaches back

threads the idea of the boat to the idea of water
chores here are choral

the chords of your work connect you
crouched in the shade, dustpan in hand

if lingering is the wind
if the waves of the sky-road are really wind

water is waves
if the boat sails through mist

will the island coalesce
will you coalesce

of dust and light and broken glass

who has to sweep
who has to patch the empty frame

who is going to fly back
to blue

SLEEP DOOR

a light knocking on the sleep door
like the sound of a rope striking the side of a boat

heard underwater
boats pulling up alongside each other

beneath the surface we rub up against each other
will we capsize in

the surge and silence
of waking from sleep

you are a lost canoe, navigating by me
I am the star map tonight

all the failed echoes
don't matter

the painted-over murals
don't matter

you can find your way to me
by the faint star-lamp

we are a fleet now
our prows zeroing in

praying in the wind
to spin like haywire compasses

toward whichever direction
will have us

GARLAND

The *mala* around your wrist is meant
to remind you to go back to the stone-year.

When you were cold, locked out,
cocooned, no one called.

Tone deaf and friendless, you decided:
less collage, more song.

More song meant you got limber,
abandoned the agreed-upon ocean.

You remember it as difficult,
but that part was easy.

If time can unmoor itself and cast off,
so can you—

RAMADAN

You wanted to be so hungry, you would break into branches,
and have to choose between the starving month's

nineteenth, twenty-first, and twenty-third evenings.
The liturgy begins to echo itself and why does it matter?

If the groundwater is too scarce one can stretch nets
into the air and harvest the fog.

Hunger opens you to illiteracy,
thirst makes clear the starving pattern,

the thick night is so quiet, the spinning spider pauses,
the angel stops whispering for a moment—

The secret night could already be over,
you will have to listen very carefully—

You are never going to know which night's mouth is sacredly reciting
and which night's recitation is secretly mere wind—

URSA MAJOR

dear mother in the sky
unbuckle the book

and erase all
the annotations

you could suckle or
suffocate me

how will you find
the little polar star in

the vast sky disowned
from his constellation

blinking at you across
unspeakable distance

THE NINTH PLANET

In the shadow cast by the end of time,
who would believe the earth was not merely a vast plain.

Faith requires laws to seize control,
and assure clay's obedience to gravity and light.

Who wouldn't believe that otherwise we wouldn't slingshot
into space, that oceans wouldn't pour from the earth's stark edges?

The universe is the most human of individuals:
Lowell never saw the proof of Pluto in his lifetime—

observing an erratic wobble in Neptune's orbit,
he plotted diagrams and equations,

left detailed instructions as to where in the night sky
the last once-wanderer would be found

DEAR LANTERN, DEAR CUP

should You light the way
or should You hold me

dear earthquake in the ground
who is waiting

am I shining into infinite space
or will I be spilled

NAVAL MISSIVE

Will I ever dare to pray for something real or will I stay at the sill,
looking out, wanting to know who is looking back.

I write archives into letters folded as boats,
dropped into the stream at midnight.

Drifting somewhere between map and maelstrom,
should I ask for my thirst to be quenched or for unquenchable thirst?

AUGUST

A jigsaw of nothing but sky
Three pieces next to one another
A clamor, a lull, an official complaint
No map provides for sore spots or depths
Not an ounce of white in sight
You're unlocatable
Three different versions of downpour
A trembling instrument
When the wait was empty
Music came out of the woods
Not what you expected
An empty place and no piece to match
How could you turn into blue
What in the world were you doing
When the picture was shown
You receive no image or instruction
What you seek to fit into does not cease

PERISH

What I am frightened of night

Twelve voices that cannot manage harmony

Segovia's technique in which the last two fingers pluck

The chapter that's the heart of *Moby-Dick*

Sounds different in the wild

An utterly different pair of strings

That vibrate on their own

Tashtego drowning in sperm oil

Mathematicians in Egypt make precise calculations

Once sung by a single human voice

To relocate all the temples endangered by the dam's construction

Carried by his friend out of danger and back aboard

PIP

He slips between the pages
into depth

Is this what was written
on the body's blank

Who you're praying to
is perhaps

A castaway: lost in publication,
unfinished

The boats mount their
horizonward search

I do not want to drown or
be lost rather

In blue smoke, a sound of
oars working

My name being
called

AUTOBIOGRAPHY

we didn't really speak but
my summer wants to answer

the architecture doesn't matter
this is not my real life

when I am here I want to know
why do I believe what I was taught

a storm is on the way
close all the windows

begin at the earliest hour
is there a self

WAITING FOR THE TRAIN

who are you perfect wind

clarinet or oboe

Friday working out a methodology of weather

waiting for the train it pleases me to listen

or to look west

water splashing the pier, a car door slams

breeze goes right into my ears

background noise but to what

that there might be a wood-spider on the back of my neck

I am brief and a river

somehow space and far away

after opening my eyes the afternoon becomes blue

birds a breathtaking conference

life while the noise stills uncertain

uncertain the worrisome adversary

or am I the adversary racing for shore

arrangement of birds or a raiment

arraignment of the river for mouthing off

am I music or motion—

the question on which the wind lectures me all afternoon

o

FROM

BRIGHT
FELON

o

MARBLE HILL

Paradise lies beneath the feet of your mother. A verse I've heard recited so frequently I do not know if it is scripture or *hadith*.

Hadith, meaning traditions of the prophet, are always accompanied by a careful oral lineage of who said what to whom, and who heard who say they heard what. Usually back to one of the prophet's wives who heard the prophet say it.

The veil also between what you want to see and cannot see, what you wish to have heard but did not hear.

In *butoh* the dancers are rendered in white smoke, ghosts traversing the stage-as-womb, moving so slowly you do not even know they are there.

If paradise lies beneath the feet of my mother then how will I find my way inside unless she admits me.

Now I look at each face, each body, as it moves around the subway platform, down the stairs and around the platform, onto trains, off of them.

After my aunt Chand-Mumani's death I thought of them each as flames, in each the body is combusting, burning up the fuel of the soul.

Michelle after giving birth walked around the city imagining everyone glistening, bordered in amniotic grit.

But is it really like Fanny writes, the body only a car the soul is driving.

Or something of us sunk into the matter of the body, part of us actually flesh, inseparable from it and upon death, truly dispersed, smoke.

The body of the prophet's wife always between us. Who said what.

In which case there really is something to grieve at death: that the soul is wind, not immortal.

A middle-aged woman, in the seat in front of me on the train, wearing a green puffy winter jacket. Her hair, though pulled back, frizzy and unkempt.

It's the unkempt I feel tenderness towards.

Have always felt about myself a messiness, an awkwardness, an ugliness.

As a child, such an envy of birds, of graceful slopes, of muscular boys.

In the train rushing above ground at 125th Street. Thinking about stumbling.

House by house, walking down this street or the other one. Going into the library, going into the school.

Where every middle-aged woman is my mother.

Waiting to be trusted with the truth.

I have nearly as much silver in my hair as she does.

Any pronoun here can be misread. He can mean you can mean I.

An odd list of things I want to do in the next five years: Study *butoh*. Write an autobiography. Go back to Paris. Get lost somewhere I haven't been.

Also begin to say it.

Marco and I moved to Marble Hill in the summer of 2006.

Let me tell you a story about a city that floats into the ocean. Opposite of Atlantis which fell into the sea or Cascadia which threatens to rise back out of it.

Marble Hill, a real hill, perched at the northernmost tip of Manhattan Island, a promontory out into the conjunction of the Hudson River and Spuyten Duyvil Creek.

The wind is an instrument, its own section of the sky orchestra.

Today I read of a Turkish mullah who is canceling 800 different *hadith* regarding treatment of women found now or believed at least to be untrue.

Untrue is it.

Untrue the laws that were graven in fire or graven in stone.

Says the Qur'an, "This is the Book. In it there is no doubt."

All for a belief that a human animal is a wicked one and requires a law.

Which requires if not actual violence then at least the threat of it.

At least fury.

Here in Marble Hill you are where you aren't.

Orchestral the river that curves and curves north of the island.

Ships bound for the upper east side from Albany have a harder and harder time negotiating the torturous and twisting Spuyten Duyvil.

So a canal is blasted through and what was once the northern tip of Manhattan became an island.

Walking across one of the bridges in Paris I came to a place called Les Mauvaises Garçons. Being afraid to enter I crossed the street to another tavern.

I stayed for three hours.

Radiant with traffic, the streets do not remember the gone.

The pillar at the Place de la Bastille does not put back brick or bar.

Ten miles out of Chartres nothing but grain across and gray above a dark raven emerges screaming from the fields.

These thoughts are nothing, following one after the other.

Somali lesbians scheduled for their execution. Two boys in Iran convicted of drunken and lewd behavior and hanged for it. Boys. 16 and 18. There was video footage of the actual hanging on the internet.

I watched it myself.

"You wear your fingers down copying sacred texts," sang Lalla, "but still the rage inside you has found no way to leave."

The Arabic line "This is the Book. In it there is no doubt" can also be read as "This is, no doubt, the Book . . ."

Dear mother, there is a folder of my loose poems lost somewhere during the summer of 2006 when I traveled between Pennsylvania, New York City, Virginia, Maine, and your house in Buffalo. There was a letter inside the folder to you.

Though I've looked and looked and failed to find it, I am sure it is still in the house in Buffalo somewhere. An envelope with a folder inside. Inside the folder loose poems. Tucked into poems, there was a letter.

The veil between what you want to see and what you cannot see.

Emily Dickinson sent her first letter to Thomas Higginson unsigned. She included with the unsigned letter a smaller sealed envelope in which there was a calling card upon which she had written her name.

When Colin Powell spoke at the UN about the invasion of Iraq, workers were asked to hang a black drape over Picasso's *Guernica*.

Which would have otherwise been in the background, surrounding him, as he spoke.

There is a body and a boy between you and utterance, the boy you were who could never speak.

Bright red bracelet of time.

"Fury" is how Galway Kinnell explained Dickinson's intent in writing her poems.

Poetry and fury in the time of war. Civil War for her.

What is my war? Not the one you think.

I won't say.

Constant state, sure as the white noise on the television after the station has gone off the air.

But who goes off the air any more.

And whose air.

Came to Marble Hill then.

Each night sleep is pierced by someone outside gunning their car engine over and over again before driving off.

A car alarm or two.

There is a streetlight outside the window that shines into the bedroom, bright as the moon but more orange.

Orange like the saffron scarf I wore to Tokudo. — "leaving home." When Ansho became a monk and took a new name.

The day I sat down next to a young man with a sweet smile. A gardener. Name of Marco.

The train runs the next block over. We are on the second floor so hear it if we really pay attention.

By now its rumble on the tracks, the chiming when the doors are about to close, are on the order of background noise.

I have not yet learned how to sleep through the night.

Marble Hill was an island for twenty years before the Spuyten Duyvil Creek, still running, underground below 228th Street, was filled in and joined to the mainland.

The city itself, my life, that first *butoh* performance I saw.

A man with such slow and intense movements, so internal.

You hardly knew he had moved at all and suddenly he was all the way across the stage, contorted, holding a glass bowl aloft in which a fish swam.

None of which you had even noticed was on the stage.

As I write this, a car alarm. The train.

Then silence.

CARLISLE

Because what I think is that this tender beast, brown-skinned animal grotesque and lustful, is me and my immortal soul besides.

In Carlisle I have two writing desks on opposite sides of the room, one the pecan-wood desk with the nicks on the thin legs, the deer legs. The other a butler-desk with grille-covered bookshelves built into the sides.

Both of these I bought with money from my first real job when I moved north of the city to Rhinebeck.

A part of the story I haven't gotten to yet. Though it was already years ago.

Always in the broken story there is more to tell.

Mornings I rise in the cold and walk two blocks down to the old colonial graveyard to read history in the broken stones, names sometimes worn away, the stories of first wives, second wives, dead infants and unmarked whose.

In this way read the history of the place.

The history of any place for me is simple: a route between my home on South Bedford Street, across the main intersection, called "the Square," to the coffee shop on the corner of Pitt and High Street.

The other compass points are the independent bookstore, the used bookstore, a house on Hanover Street where Marianne Moore lived, and a strange park that was once a graveyard.

On the north side of town, a place where the land was broken and bones disturbed.

Details on the display plaques in that park are sketchy and will lead me into shadowed places—town records, rooms I've never been.

But I don't discover this small park near the railroad tracks with its distressing history until I've lived in the town more than seven months.

In the body of a tree I hear a resonance. While out in space between planets lie cores of planets.

An iron fence grows through the heart of the tree; I pass it every day in the morning when I walk.

You were saying something.

You hardly pass a night that winter without sneaking out into the hallway and turning the thermostat up four or five degrees.

Eating baked beans out of a can with couscous for dinner nearly every night. Not because you live alone or don't have the time to take care of yourself better.

But because you like the taste of it.

What I learned is that each asteroid is held in careful place by a partner in space. If such a body didn't exist the orbital patterns of these same can be extrapolated graphically.

A discovery which pleases me almost as much as when I learned that every cubic equation has an associated modular form.

But is the reverse true.

And what has all this to do with.

Carlisle, Pennsylvania. Once a frontier town. But constructed at the frontier with specific intent.

To push the boundaries of the state out to the Cumberland Pass.

I wrote an autobiography once in letters. To someone. In which I found myself unable to actually say anything so I tried saying it in two or three or four different versions. Eventually leaving all the various versions in.

Called it *The Historical Need for Music*. Or was that *Hysterical Need*.

Repeating the chapters in different variations so I could speak out of both sides of my mouth, not because I wanted to evade but because I didn't know what really happened.

The County Jail, gothic, redstone, still stands at the corner of Bedford and High Streets though is offices now, the insides completely refurbished with industrial gray carpeting, drop ceilings, and fluorescent lights.

You have to squint at it to be fearful, though death it still tells—a white man crushed in riots when he tried to sue for the return of two of his slaves that had escaped north.

Needing to check whether or not he won his case. The question of "law" vs. "morality" being what interests me.

To live in a frontier town at any rate or a town that was built on what was supposed to be the frontier.

Later all the promises were broken and the settlements spread into the territories.

It's always the broken that holds the universe in place.

That's what I would say about poetry and prayer.

That god or audience—the intended direction of both of those—we wish and wish are real.

In the mornings of the late fall when it is cold enough to feel the winter beginning I would leave the house very early and walk south on Bedford Street into the old cemetery.

Here's the closest place you come in America to a city piled on top of a city.

Not like that in Cairo where the city sedimented itself and we walked down the Greek streets themselves, saw the churches hidden underground, accessible only by otherwise unmarked staircases in empty courtyards.

Through the cemetery I read the fate of the village, the deaths, the family trees, the broken headstones. How we will all break.

When I speak about my body's life I know it is brothered and descended from but do not know if blood will descend from my blood.

Does a family break or can it like water evaporate and condense and so will I then be a father in a million different ways.

Leaving the cemetery I walk through the old districts to the north side of town and after crossing the railroad tracks find a park there which is really another cemetery.

Or was—the graves now all dug up, replaced by a small green park.

One grave surrounded by a small iron fence remains. The granddaughter of this man lived across the street and when the park was planned she battled to have this grave protected and so it was.

The others, descendantless, have disappeared, the headstones, shattered and removed, the ground planted over.

As I walk I realize, likely the bodies and bones remain, deep underground, dissipating.

You know without explanation whose graveyard that was that was torn up. You understand the color of their skin that enabled their desecration and what station they occupied in this community while they lived.

Why should I spell out every little thing.

There are things about a person's body you do not know, the things it craves and loves. All the sordid things we could never tell, the cheap things, tawdry and paltry.

Carlisle where soldiers are trained and so-called "Indians" were brought to be forced to forget.

Never did I think when I arrived there that it would be the place I would sort myself out and dare actually to speak.

Nothing happened there but time.

Going in the morning to the coffee shop to read or to write.

How ordinary the most important things are.

The green copper roofs of the buildings against the steel blue-gray of the Central Pennsylvania sky. You could look at anything and understand.

In the sky, in the rain-wet street, in the palm of your hand.

Is always what you promised. What you promised is to understand.

Maybe you're never going to get there.

I thought I wouldn't get there unless I spoke, unless I told about the people I loved, the picture I drew against the corner of the room.

I'm trying to tell you how ridiculously hard it was to even try to open my mouth, to make words let alone sentences. How silence can fill every space.

To drown in a river or to lift the water up and let the drowning be your guide.

I trudge along the street unbaptized and criminal according to some religious laws.

Lonely brother, middle child, only son.

Is it written on your skin, my friend asks. Is that why you could never go on pilgrimage, never go to Mecca.

Why is it I would want go to Mecca. Because there a stone fell from the sky.

But more importantly than that small thing. That is where a mother refused to believe.

A mother refused to believe the obvious: I am alone in the desert with my son.

His breath rattles in his throat.

We have been left here by the patriarch who promised to return.

Sound familiar.

He left us and we were promised by god to safety.

This is the question of faith on the frontier.

You were promised deliverance yet there you are, no water in sight.

Do you sit and wait for the angel to either spell it all out into your ears or perhaps write it onto your skin.

Yet I think it is already written on my face, written into every corner as many times as I could say it.

There must be water around here somewhere.

Yet it isn't panic to leave a baby even then in the moment of dying.

Isn't. Is it.

And that's how it happened. God wouldn't spell it out.

Rather the water came exactly where she put the boy down.

After she risked it all for the impossible: water in the desert.

In the desert the mother was left.

She had to decide.

Do you wait for god to tell you what to do.

Or do you panic.

CAIRO

In Egypt I asked why words exist we cannot pronounce. Asked as
Egyptian people mispronounced words like: Egypt. Pyramid. Sphinx.

Where are you from, the young tourist-police official asks me at the gate
of the Egyptian Museum.

The guard looks so young—he's a boy of seventeen or eighteen, a black
machine gun slung over his shoulder.

I am Indian, I say, nervous by how close his face is to mine.

If you are Indian, he says slowly, leaning closer, putting his hand on my
bare upper arm, where is your elephant.

I do not know any of the rules of communication here. Is he flirting with
me. Am I danger. Or is he trying to be funny or friendly.

In the one place everyone looks like me—has my name—I am the most
foreign.

An eternal sense: ever since there's been history, a telling of what
happened, there have been people who have lived at this river, at this
place.

The city as we drove from the airport seemed to become
monstrous—from the plane it stretched horizon to horizon.

The cities of the past—all built geographically on top of each other, but
also historically, culturally, linguistically.

There is no such thing as a "present" moment, nor "of this city."

The people I see walking down the street exactly resemble the figures in the papyrus paintings, in the carvings.

As it comes close to opening time, the workers begin to disappear to their jobs—the security guards, with black-irised eyes and long lashes, dressed in bright white, hefting their black guns casually, unbelievably young, remain on every corner.

This book is sewn together. I am without language. The streets are so busy, how will I get across the river?

The week before I left for Egypt I took the fast-boat from Boston to Provincetown. The boat was going so quickly it skipped on the surface of the water.

I've come to forget the years of joy.

You've a thread, lost in a labyrinth.

You will drink from the river.

In the labyrinth the creature becomes not itself.

You've forgotten the thread, bull-man, wolf-man, fox-man . . .

There is a river in the labyrinth, Nile or Hudson or anything else you can name.

In Clarence once, at the height of winter, the snow two feet deep, seventeen wild turkeys picking their way through the yard, heading towards the house.

A labyrinth of time ties you back to the streets of Cairo, months after fifty-two men were arrested on a floating nightclub, taken to jail for crimes against society. Their trials will stretch out.

For years.

Such is the wandering and searching for the shining thread.

You will not forget the way out.

You will forget the way out.

In Paris I first saw the work of Nicolas de Staël. In Egypt I wished I thought of him.

"One simply cannot think of any object whatsoever, because there are simultaneously so many objects that the ability to take them in falters and fades," wrote de Staël.

I never knew if a bird was history or pharaonic. Never knew pyramid or the glass lid of the bottle.

Held at the center of the hotel like a prisoner.

What willful or wander waited.

Evening. At Stonecrop Gardens. Marco and I had dinner at Café Maya. Earlier we walked through the gardens, down the Himalayan slope, to the Bamboo grove.

How can I pick poems other than by heart? What do I really want to share with people? Not of my methods but of myself?

It's strange to look at what I've chosen for the manuscript I'm calling "the Far Mosque," sliced up, divorced from all the hundreds of other pages that went along with it. It feels like an excerpt of a book that never existed.

As if I ever existed.

Egypt was a concept or a country. I never saw it, never took the bus down the river to Alexandria, never wondered.

After *The Far Mosque* was published I learned about the controversy: whether the actual Al-Aqsa in Jerusalem is the "far mosque" of the legend, being described only by its adjective.

It didn't matter according to Rumi, who said something like, "the farthest mosque is the one within."

Days I wandered on my own; Salah, the driver assigned by the company to my father took me where I wanted to go.

Mohammed, the Egyptian man with an Austrian mother sat with me in the steam room of the hotel.

Salah took me to Cairo Tower, to the museums, offered to take me to the Sunni mosques and for some reason I did not want to go.

In the ether time of my childhood when I learned to speak I learned to recite syllables whose meaning I do not know.

Any teacher of a sacred text will tell you when he's teaching you that pronunciation is of utmost importance and that the power of the word is inherent in the unknown language itself.

Why, for example, *namaaz* must be recited in Arabic or the vedantic chants spoken in Sanskrit. Or the Torah be recited in Hebrew.

It is not a mere theoretical distrust of translation but another form of distance from G—D, who if truly omnipotent or omnipresent must exist without language, which even in its mortal form functions as a form of distance—necessary perhaps—from meaning.

I am on a rescue mission.

Dad and I went to the Coptic Quarter, down the narrow stone streets we make our way into a churchyard with no church.

In the subterranean church I wondered and fumbled for my father's hand.

Where are we and who are we.

Nine days later down the coast of dark countries, threaded by the wheeling stars, angel undone, light comes up.

The light opened onto shores and not onto open sea.

What shores are these.

The stars will not say.

Misread the characters of my name; for "patience" read "generous" or "divided."

The terrain shifts to thunderous mountains.

This is where you forgot yourself.

Where you slept for twenty years.

Storm clouds gather and settle along peaks.

The air is liquid with jags of lightning.

You are a sleeping rosetta slid between the liquid lightning and stone peak.

Wake up wake up cross the bridge into another country.

We took the car down to Saqqara one day where there is a step pyramid, older than the three at Giza.

The entrance through the Temple of the Sun, which having no roof now is truer to its function as a ruin than ever as a temple.

As I stood in the sand-yard in front of the pyramid soaring above into the pale blue desert sky I looked west into the dune.

The desert in that direction stretches thousands of miles, all the way to the Atlantic.

A pit is so deep I cannot see the bottom in the ruined city of the wind.

Monument wake to me what is ancient and built.

Were we there.

I uncover a layer of hieroglyphics at the bottom of the wall, clearing sand away.

Every tomb has a watchman.

That magnificent pale, dusty blue sky. The color otherwise only ochre.

Imagining the previous life in the city behind the pyramid, not a necropolis but the ruined walls and foundations of an ancient city, a city before this place was desert.

Dreaming of the sweet watermelon from breakfast.

Rameses broken, lying down in the eroded empire, ringed by European and Japanese tourists on the second floor, looking over the railing.

It keeps these monuments in the immediate present—sacrilege also the way we walked amongst them, graffiti-scarred, people touching everything . . .

Hard to discern what was original and what was reinforced construction.

In this way the ancient is lashed to the present but simultaneously kept ancient for public consumption.

I feel I am wandering a labyrinth but without a center, a bull, a thread.

The terrific beauty of the young man in the church, sitting in the pew next to me, his hand resting lightly on his leg, the violence with which the priest took the candles of the schoolboys and blew them out.

Earlier as we were driving through the valley to the beautiful beginning of Memphis I thought: here is the ancient kingdom of Kemet—just beyond Saqqara, the desert's edge—the magnificent first view of the kingdom from the desert.

On the way back from Cairo several workers were taking turns swinging from a tree into the river. I watched one, laughing, shaking his dark curls, grasp the rope and swing wild over the water. His white shirt wet against his chest.

I have to be able to say it.

In June of 2001 I went to Cairo, Egypt. All this was written during a decade of nearly continuous air raids and bombing of Iraq, the birthplace of civilization and of written language.

Osiris was torn into pieces by his brother; Isis traveled the world in search of the fragments to reassemble him.

And they said: oh Lord make spaces to be longer between our journeys . . . so We made them stories and scattered them with terrible scattering . . . most surely there are Signs in this for every patient grateful one (Qur'an 34:19)

Layla al-Attar, the Iraqi painter, was killed when her house was struck by one of twenty-three Tomahawk missiles President Clinton launched at Baghdad in June of 1993 in retaliation for an alleged previously planned attempt on President Bush's life. Details of that plot have never been uncovered or proven. Al-Attar's home was reduced to rubble, her husband killed, her daughter blinded, and much of her work destroyed.

The libraries of Baghdad disappear into flame and smoke. The clay tablets smashed. Qur'ans burning.

I am writing you this from the past—

From "Thorow" by Susan Howe: *And what is left when spirits have fled from holy places?*

Valley riven the early year. Shift the plates and carve.

Cairo: an ancient statue of the Pharaoh next to statues of revolutionary heroes of the twentieth century.

An old Coptic church near an Arab mosque built over Greek ruins.

A ruined Roman aqueduct threads its way from the Nile to the citadel of the Turks.

Howe: *I thought I stood on the shores of a history of the world where forms of wildness brought up by memory become desire and multiply.*

Yet the hieroglyph does not unfigure. At a time when brutal strategy is employed in a war against the Arab people in the name of Western financial interests I went into the city looking for untranslatable icons.

The Egyptian people, having Arab tongues, cannot correctly pronounce particular words tied into their mouths: *Pyramid. Sphinx. Egypt.*

My language buckled into my mouth, unbuckled itself.

Howe: *In the machinery of injustice my whole being is Vision.*

Faltering perhaps, fading for sure, though I mispronounce myself, I will speak.

PARIS

Your little canvas, *a little autobiography littered on the surface.* The way you first started swearing: on your back on the stone fence in Cassis, overlooking the stretch of mountains into the water to the calanques that spell you.

Fingers spell down your back.

Or spill.

Taking the night boat to Corsica, waking up in another country.

Drunk year, stone year, tell it all backwards so what's before comes after.

You'll manage it that way.

I came to believe when I went into the cathedral of Chartres, raven in the field, to see the Veil of the Virgin. Came to believe the point is not to see through the thing that separates us but that the thing itself that separates is part of the point.

Coming through the dark crowds I thought to myself it was a hoax, the foot of a saint or something like that.

I said if it is fake it will be rich, blue velvet, embroidered with stars, but if it is real—

Struck the sun sinking, the trees amber, ember of flowers, the membrane of skin, the stains of last year's yearning, an urge of opening, on the verge of saying—

What must such a cloth look like.

Blue long since faded, embroidered stars unraveled.

In the wind along the road to Chartres, but here too—where's here—or on the walk through the Camargue from Arles to the sea.

White threads reaching backwards.

Catherine tells about her pilgrimage from Paris to Chartres following the medieval route, some pilgrims walking, in the old custom, on their knees.

There, on Tuesday, between a raven screaming from the fields and a walk through the cold labyrinth, and a bowl of garlic soup, I wanted to see not through but at the veil itself.

I threaded my way through cities, from bookshop to bookshop, church to church, and museum to museum.

How could I have come there and not believed.

At the chapel of Jeanne in the nave, a stone eagle bends to pluck grapes, saints lining the spires.

Unwell at the chapel of Jeanne, lighting candles, in the dark recess two ghosts.

One says "Are you brave enough."

I could not say, I could not say.

The river moves too quickly, separated stream from bank.

In the shadows, bank of material for prayers: 5 francs for a candle.

At the chapel of the thirteenth apostle the sun comes through the broken rose of lead and sand.

Thirteenth station of the cross the hand is cut on the candle, a jeweled box holding the bones of a British princess, Saint Ursule, splintered.

Dirt in my hands, dirt in my mouth.

What is the sound of blood vessels ripping away from bone, the breaking of the casket, the walls of the cathedral held up by thin shafts, iron straps of a ship trembling.

What is that sound we should not remember.

Braque: *La vase donne une forme au vide et la musique au silence.*

Novemberlight bent sideways and down, this is July walking down Champ de Mars to the water. A portrait painter on the bridge.

There on a small island, near Bartholdi's small model of the Liberty, I began writing in my journal in French, for five pages I wrote but only in the vocabulary I understood.

When I next switched back to English I found myself confounded by the boundary of the French in my head—unable to write more complexly than what I could express in the foreign language.

The condition followed me south on the train into the mountains of Corsica and back to New York.

It wasn't until years after that, when everyone started speaking in tongues that I.

Came to the house at Giverny to speak in tongues. In the morning we saw the scorched cathedral of Rouen.

Ruined. A gate to the garden, on the surface of the pond a dark shine.

The windows of the cathedral had all shattered during the war and been replaced by clear panes, the nave flooded by light.

Underneath the shine in the garden of a painter, a better pilgrimage site than any other, I stay on the bridge, wait for the dark to rise up, cover the paths. Pull the house down.

In the Quartier Latin I wondered what quarter has torn. Feeling in pieces, I mean and not knowing why.

The streets break for the river, the river cut in the shape of an angel, an angel in the shape of the wings of a river, a halo of light.

Harsh rain strafing leaves from the trees, birds unwrapping from the rain-slick eaves.

But I am hardly at the beginning of what I want to tell you.

When I went into the meditation room with its white walls I lost track of sound in the hum.

I wrote letters on my arms and my ankles. How the body pulls long to look for a poem.

What poem in the afternoon, sitting at the bridge watching the river travel underneath.

Is that all there is to it, that and languages I don't understand.

Because one day, a winter afternoon, one day in seven years I am going to find myself mapping out the spaces into which I never spoke.

I will not only be saying it in the present but will be saying it backwards and forwards.

Ahead, the new world where I am going to find for myself, completely consequenceless and inconsequential.

But also the lonely one who wandered from rue Tiphaine to Champ de Mars, from Champ de Mars to Trocadéro, down the rue des Eaux he dared himself.

Dared himself into the future to find himself, to say what he wanted, say who he loved.

He wouldn't speak and instead watched the wooden struts of the town break and disappear into the waters.

Imagine watching the town break and the small buildings fold down.

Paradise lies beneath the feet of your mother or does Paradise lie at all.

Paradise the perfect painting, the panel is unmarked, surrounded by dried leaves.

In smoke a figure moves, bright orange trees, mauve beaches, great blocks of color.

Behind the figure, sharp flashes of light, behind the light, rising emerald, a hillside studded with lemons.

This is you, a mirror caked in clear varnish.

You in the morning walking along the river.

For what have you come?

In the evening thinking about the day. *What did you see? What did you say?*

Clamping your hand over your mouth.

What did you think you would find here so far from your life?

This is you whispering into your own ear.

This is you refusing to hear.

If all the tongues fade to background noise you're left with what.

An idea you have to choose between one thing and another, between them hanging the veil, the syllable of your life you cannot pronounce.

Over the stone wall, sprays of fuchsia, the wind is cold and beautiful and you've walked too far away from the apartment.

What a battle in your mouth, washed in the evening.

Still the door is unlatched, the evening light left on.

Don't tell yet about when you spoke, about when you were told about your crime, punishable according to some, by death.

At the Rodin Museum you had no money and tried to trick your way inside to those rooms full of figures emerging alive from marble.

You never got as far as the front door.

But linger in the garden

Sand marks the footfall, the approach to the great iron door.

And you start whispering, though too late, too late, *your back is a nation I have not visited . . .*

The sculptor with his dusty hands, mallet and chisel, a prisoner in bronze and black iron, a door to hell.

The light shines through the twisting figures.

One of them asks are you brave enough. To walk through the door to fire.

And what of the part of the sculpture which has been cut away.

What still of the rock left unquarried in the earth.

HOME

My father had a steel comb with which he would comb our hair.

After a bath the cold metal soothing against my scalp, his hand cupping my chin.

My mother had a red pullover with a little yellow duck embroidered on it and a pendant made from a gold Victoria coronation coin.

Which later, when we first moved to Buffalo, would be stolen from the house.

The Sunni Muslims have a story in which the angels cast a dark mark out of Prophet Muhammad's heart, thus making him pure, though the Shi'a reject this story, believe in his absolute innocence from birth.

Telling the famous Story of the Blanket in which the Prophet covers himself with a Yemeni blanket for his afternoon rest. Joined under the blanket first by by his two grandchildren Hassan and Hussain, then by his son-in-law Ali, and finally by his daughter Bibi Fatima.

In Heaven, Gabriel asks God about the five under the blanket and God says, those are the five people whom I loved the most out of all creation and I made everything in the heavens and the earth for their sake.

Gabriel, speaker on God's behalf, whisperer to Prophets, asks God, can I go down and be the sixth among them.

And God says, go down there and ask them. If they consent you may go under the blanket and be the sixth among them.

Creation for the sake of Gabriel is retroactively granted when the group under the blanket admits him to their company.

Is that me at the edge of the blanket asking to be allowed inside.

Asking that eight hundred hadith be canceled, all history re-ordered.

In Hyderabad I prayed every part of the day, climbed a thousand steps to the site of Maula Ali's pilgrimage.

I wanted to be those stairs, the hunger I felt, the river inside.

I learned to pronounce my daily prayers from transliterated English in a book called *Know Your Islam*, dark blue with gold calligraphed writing that made the English appear as if it were Arabic complete with marks above and below the letters.

I didn't learn the Arabic script until years later and never learned the language itself.

God's true language: Hebrew. Latin. Arabic. Sanskrit.

As if utterance fit into the requirements of the human mouth.

I learned how to find the new moon by looking for the dark absence of stars.

When Abraham took Isaac up into the thicket his son did not know where he was being led.

When his father bound him and took up the knife he was shocked.

And said, "Father, where is the ram?"

Though from Abraham's perspective he was asked by God to sacrifice his son and he proved his love by taking up the knife.

Thinking to himself perhaps, Oh Ishmael, Ishmael, do I cut or do I burn.

I learned God's true language is only silence and breath.

Fourth son of a fourth son, my father was afflicted as a child and as was the custom in those days a new name was selected for him to protect his health.

Still the feeling of his rough hand, gently cupping my cheek, dipping the steel comb in water to comb my hair flat.

My hair was kept so short, combed flat when wet. I never knew my hair was wavy until I was nearly twenty-two and never went outside with wet and uncombed hair until I was twenty-eight.

At which point I realized my hair was curly.

My father's hands had fortune-lines in them cut deeply and dramatic.

The day I left his house for the last time I asked him if I could hold his hand before I left.

There are two different ways of going about this.

If you have known this for years why didn't you ask for help, he asked me.

Each time I left home, including the last time, my mother would hold a Qur'an up for me to walk under. Once under, one would turn and kiss the book.

There is no place in the Qur'an which requires acts of homosexuality to be punishable by lashings and death.

Hadith or scripture. Scripture or rupture.

Should I travel out from under the blanket.

Comfort from a verse which also recurs: "Surely there are signs in this for those of you who would reflect."

Or the one hundred and four books of God. Of which only four are known—*qur'aan, injeel, tavrat, zubuur.*

There are a hundred others—*Bhaghavad-Gita, Lotus Sutra, Song of Myself, the Gospel of Magdalen, Popul Vuh, the book of Black Buffalo Woman*—somewhere unrevealed as such.

Dear mother in the sky you could unbuckle the book and erase all the annotations.

What I always remember about my childhood is my mother whispering to me, telling me secrets, ideas, suggestions.

She named me when I moved in her while she was reading a calligraphy of the Imam's names. My name: translated my whole life for me as *Patience.*

In India we climbed the steps of the Maula Ali mountain to the top, thirsting for what.

My mother had stayed behind in the house, unable to go on pilgrimage. She had told me the reason why.

Being in a state considered unacceptable for prayers or pilgrimages.

I asked if she would want more children and she told me the name she would give a new son.

I always attribute the fact that they did not, though my eldest sister's first son was given the same name she whispered to me that afternoon, to my telling of her secret to my sisters when we were climbing the stairs.

It is the one betrayal of her—perhaps meaningless—for which I have never forgiven myself.

There are secrets it is still hard to tell, betrayals hard to make.

You hope like anything that though others consider you unclean God will still welcome you.

My name is Kazim. Which means *patience*. I know how to wait.

o

FROM

SKY

WARD

o

DIVINATION

Your son turns restive in his sleep
Whispered away by morning to dusk

Verses bloom along his wrists and throat
In bright sentences his name is cut

Five times a day he cries out
His voice snuffed in flowery wells

He knows in his heart none can take you truly in
Save the house that unhomed you

FAIRY TALE

In the acres of garden before an empty house an amnesiac prince collects broken branches, prunes the fruit trees, plucks weeds from the rock bed.

He speaks a broken language of beach and Broadway and on the way to shore gets lost and finds himself in a cemetery at sunset, pink light on the stones.

He cannot read the inscriptions but kneels down at a cenotaph anyhow and recites the only prayers he can remember.

Why, when we wanted to speak to nothing but water, is he singing verses down into the stone-hard earth in a town he has never belonged to, lost on his way to the shore?

If only he would learn to read the book of the sky, he would see the birds circling lazily around hot currents, which could only mean a large body of water is near.

The words are hollow in his mouth and he doesn't know what he believes anyhow, whether bodies will again rise or if the aerial rumors of the gulls will lead him to the sea or if the numb tombstone in his mouth might indeed one day speak.

His scripture comes out sideways and his mispronunciation of the most sacred of syllables makes him always friendless. It's nearly a party trick the way he opens his mouth and butterflies pour out, closes it again and the clock chimes, reminding him of being a young boy, coming home to an empty house, sure that he had been forgotten, that everyone had gone to the beach without him.

Sure that he would always be forgotten, that he would lie down in his grave and no ghost would come to fetch him or explain god or what was supposed to happen next.

That the grave would fill with dirt and he would rise on the boat of his body. That no one would recite sacred chapters for him, that he wouldn't know how to take the rudder, that the sea was too far.

The boat now coming apart, his voice dwindling, hard as stone.

Finally he sees a bird winging down calling, "Find-me, find-me!"

But he doesn't understand words, only sound, the shape of words, the tune to which they are sung.

All the sacred verses in the world are like birds wheeling in the sky, who knows where they go.

FROZEN

Daily I wish stitched here to live

Facing west watching the last light

Tattooed on my left wrist, "let-go"

Tattooed on my right wrist, "not-it"

Daily you make me dizzy with messages

Nightly torn open by brute sky and eagle claw

The strongest man in the world is on his way to release me

But what happens when a frozen man is touched by fire

Upon release I may disappear

PRAYER REQUEST CARDS

I would like the church to pray for

> a clear reckoning
> the core unearthed
> what's best born skyward
> searched

> who's most easily followed
> seared

> who's most faithful
> beckoned to
> queer

I would like the church to pray

> my psalm to unsettle the case
> my askance umbilical lust to review
> and refute the evidence

> to enter my gilt-edged tongue
> as final proof
> of innocence

I would like the church

> on the inside of my sin
> to spell out my breath
> to draw a wing

AUTOBIOGRAPHY

begin at the earliest hour
is there a self

at the corner of San Anton and Duende I hardly know
the edge of the sidewalk a bare consonant
of the city's harsh sentence

how can I say my actual name
when all I can manage is counting change
for coffee I do not buy

every night the clouds argue in the sky
for the right to be the one who will part
to reveal the new moon

blank but appearing
day by day
a new misunderstanding of gone

how can you already know if you have never yet been
the twin inside arriving after departure
the crime of history, a quivering vessel

my also bones a manic making
who am I a man inside a bell inside someone else's face
fingers that hold a skull or pen

of course a swan could be an elephant or a man could be on fire
the coffee I didn't drink is pouring through time
inside any city a thousand vowels pronounce themselves

every street map has a thousand
pointing arrows labeled
"You are here"

but who are you
at the corner of San Anton and Duende
dark-eyed and holding your empty

no body knows you
hardly arriving and
already gone

THE ESCAPE

Father whose purpose swims
while the universe mends itself

Wind was water
porpoise was prophet

Father my swim
the sutured eventual blue splinters

Seed planter, hedonist
heathen when the unwise son fell to pieces

Purposeless when the father
flew for cover

The cloven will cleave
the water finishes itself, finishes me

Stream unreeling, you are
the end of the world, an endless horizon

It's a sham, this charnel-choice
between heaven and home

Finally I am free of the labyrinth
and overhead I see nothing but sky

SINKING

you became real to me father
when I saw you fly over me from beneath the waves

a bone-white door against the cloud-white ceiling
looking for me, flapping and furious

I watched you in the dark as you slept
knowing the edge of you only by deeper darkness

below you now in the blue-black, I am a star winking out,
thinking I may wake up warm and safe in the labyrinth

and not ever do this,
not seek for the sun

oh father my storm-dark coast,
                              nothing fills

PRAYER

Denuded and abandoned I recite
but what do I want

To rise again from the ocean
or be buried alive in the surge and sleep

To be a fearsome range in a single body
or to wind my unity down into depth

Missing in action, ghost-like
bobbing in the distance

Singing psalms to terrify myself
into deciding:

So long liberation

My time in the world
Was only a gesture

My body
a lonely stranger

an ache
I never knew

RAPTURE

Here is your moment to affix me
Adoring blasphemer to breathlessness

I drop myself one by one
Back away sun and find me

Citizen of sound or stone
At the border of light clamoring

In cathedrals of menace every cruelty
Sings back to me forty voices a whole city

Devour me down and bound
Submerged just off the coast

In the battle to own yourself
Whom do you fight

Endless ocean no way now back to land
Cathedral unravel the moonless night

EPIPHANY

sky-knife open the boat to oceanic lust
I want to snake-handle but I want to be bitten

reef, ravener, revenant
remand yourselves to the undertow

sluicing from the boat edge to the self-edge
ask the wind what next blue swell

bodies unpetal to white-gray frenzy
the oar scorpions in your hand

all of us hemmed to the hull
barnacled to the underside

rain unfurling back to sky
batten me to the source

sway me dusk-crazy when you arrive

OCEAN STREET

to Alice Coltrane

blue or white or very far away
every avenue a rain-stroked aisle
through the wild wind's theater

far to the barque floating in the last row
your self laddered to an avenue of sound
last streak of white-gold found

in lines along the branches or in the branches
are you a branch that tries from the bark to speak
cold roar of the ocean you cannot speak

how loud the blue-gray morning
how loud when you dissolved yourself into sound
when you dissolved April

into the soul's endless question
what was your body but a first
uncertain answer

≈≈≈

always awakened
awakened and left

reft the wait's blue hollow
sightless an oracle trying to tell

what recedes and what's left
a shirt left crumpled in the sand

in the mist you balance on a board
the shape of a prayerbook

racing along the surface toward the rocks
finding in the water a pounding afterlife

sound that undresses itself
prayerbook spun to unravel

answering the eroding cliffs and dunes
dear orange shafts of late morning

speaking backward
and in tongues

wet-suited supplicants balancing on boards
racing for shore

how do you find your self deeply
in the forest on the ocean floor

dear snake-haired woman who wondered
to some the book in sound you wrote was thunder

it is one thing to be lost another to be left
seeking a slogan a sloka your own body

dear country-dark houseflown homewrecker
shy in the blackness telling how

you sailed again to arrive
to found yourself in sound

dear hold me seen or sign
the unsoundable notes saying

dare to leave home
drop everything

did the universe write them
or did you

every aisle a rain-stroked avenue
breathlessly quoted a letter in space
of the sea's blue promise

each spring I lie on the surface
hoping to stand aloft

my shirt crumpled in front
of the empty-hearted tree one sleeve
pointing the way to nowhere beach

wantonly disappearing every day though
I did not believe when with your breath
you made a bridge and dreamed myself wrong

my strange and weary road
my unkempt figure my blue whisper
winter god whose center

in the moment unwilling to be warm
eternal the winter eternal the wind unmaking your will

will and whisper my anger my lantern my spaceless wick
but how my tenuous prayerboard can a supplicant balancing
on the surface know anything about depth

struggling out of the waves
moon a little red illegible
whole sky starless
the late hour I didn't tell you
wrote into me the answer or a map to follow
boardless and battered
heaved ashore on the pulled-back day
in the effort of ache
where did I swim in from
water that wholly disappears into air or
does not disappear

speaking underwater because afraid to be heard
nothing after no one waiting for me
sky and sky the same grave gray that terrifies
turning the page of breath
where I left myself without sound
into the air I spell each spring like "swan"
noises from the next room keep you awake
god that was a noise in the night at the foot of the bed
claiming kinship or revival
transcribing the ghost-notes onto the sheets
we who each divine our self in spite of ourselves
running wildly boards under our arms back into the sea

in case of warmth the oceans will rise
strange cup to move through
after the continents came together

after you swam crazy through the storm to shore
after you asked for it
after you drove yourself relentlessly into the sea

we listen to one gust after the other
a gorgeous scale in the most ordinary range
drumming the time of the sea into a signature of leaves

twenty minutes of ecstasy
blue and after the blue, blue-white
a buoy, a sandpiper, a wholesale slaughter of blue

either way the harp's plucked chords
like the fog or the answer of water
dissolved into the shore's copious footnotes

transcribing the music onto ebbing surface
a missing word where continents rub together
disappear or dispel the notion
there is any such word worth knowing

a bridge collapsing along unquelled cadences of sound
when you whisper yourself to eternity
whose name did you whisper and into whose ear

blue my promise that divided itself
from flesh into sound
and from sound to womb
womb to thrum that sundered

the water's surface clamorous and racing away
dear unjacketed traveler evaporate
ghostlike distance was that you who entered
illegible annotations in my book on surf

in the tenth hour of the fourth month of which year
god the river that raced you on the surface to shore
every I a rain-stroked avenue
breathlessly quoting rain to the sand

lean close saint nothing
send me through it sister cup

a body slides through the water
cleanly angling for rocky shore
eternal internal zephyr

men have dashed themselves to death
to feel the racing thrill
how do you pronounce year after year "home" or "death"

the ocean avenue a bridge ready to collapse
pond evaporates to air
your breath made a bridge

impatient penitents race for the exit
lean close saint everyone
I live neither here nor there

the ocean scrambling itself to answer
sketching you in pieces everywhere
in an odd scene paddling against the current

straining for shore
you drew yourself in time a backwards sign
surfing on the breath

wishing to be not an echo of the ocean but its escalation
and when I cast myself across the surface I stopped wondering
would I float or would I drown

ADRIFT

Oh the diminishing racket of voices
calling my name eclipsed
by the new moon and indiscernible dark

I have somehow become the center of the universe

I wept for a year on the open water
strangling myself with banishment
sensation vanishing in the depths

the rain a faded photo from fifteen years ago

I am a forgotten bit of metropolitan trash
tied to his moment of redrawing the border
between twilight and daybreak

Forever at the edge of something that could save me

And the disastrous fear of what it would take to save me
My life in its entirety only imaginary
or perhaps the rapturous notion

I cannot be saved

PROMISEKEEPER

In the place mountains keep time as they slide into the sea
You made a promise you never kept

You fastened yourself lonely to everything that lived
Wanted to open every closed door

Wanted to turn your back on the sky
And teach yourself how to fly

Speak in the language of myth and flowers if you must
But translate it at least for the stone and dust

You built a tower to god out of bricks and mud
When you should have built it with breath

Wings will not carry you skyward
Your own body is the only mosque you need

The tongue in your mouth the only rock
From which you could ever launch yourself into heaven

THE WRESTLER

My flat breath grows flatter. Who am I now,
thick in the tricks the body plays? No matter.

The fact of this day on fire and these arms twisted
in the effort to master another

draws me in time breathless to afternoons as a boy slick
with sweat and laughter,

horizontal in a spin, one of us in control
and the other on his back and bested.

Later I would read in heaven's books
how my body was wrong, though limber and strong.

In the web of our efforts I aim to fix a position
where the other's strength ebbs and mine kicks in.

Strength splintered to pieces,
a shard in the other we each struggle to reach.

We give in turn, strip down and shift. I reach for one limb
with my right hand, grip harder to another with my left.

Our bodies flash their thunder and lack.
I strain for what I'm owed. I read heaven its riot act.

DEAR SHAMS

There's no answer to winter
sun sets over the water

falling so quickly
you have not been lost

listening for silence
where and where did you go

twelve-stringed music
rejoin me

in the sun-year I swelled long shadows
in the moon-year the valley folded itself up

you are the beloved I would not love
at the fountain witless and still

a stream pours over rocks making music
could the water rush over me

could you rush
over me

the sun drops so quickly into its banishment
could I please forget to breathe and drown

will the ocean rejoin me
you have not been lost

can I be reborn as a guitar
and you reborn as music to hum inside me

one day you stopped looking at me
and I knew

the last note was lingering in the box
of my body

you did not vanish in the marketplace
I still imagine you in me as breath

broken in thirds
corded to sound

I took your name when the sun came up
sun of winter, sun windless and wistful

come down across the water
undone sun give me the drunk go-ahead

last time I searched for you
this time I stretch hollow and resonant

last time I raved without senses
this time my angel my string-singer

pluck me oh pluck
me and hum

CONFESSION

I'm drifting now cold and stolen, the sun-bound one
Giving lie to the myth I fell

Only a story spun to warn back heathen sons
Who burn too brightly

I saw the feathers flutter down like pages
From the old man's book

Dead scared of heights
I am the wrong boy for the job of proving gravity's limit

But wings are small things invented by men
Who could not but cut the cobalt sky

From the sapphire sea
While I want to weave blue and blue together

So when the feathery pages sink
Damp beneath the waves

The ink streams clear to nothing
The story goes I drowned

Dear god, father of light
I must excuse myself from the formula

Nothing adds up to me
An equation desperate to be solved

I abandoned both wings and sun
For the blue direction

And I swear by the flowers in my mouth
I will find some place on this earth that knows me

THE PROMISE OF BLUE

What we wanted was to watch him silver fall
Cut the surface of the water and leave no bruise

Every earth bound angel who was taught his body was a sin
Calculates in his head equations needed to sculpt the air

As he aims from grim height for the promise of blue

Always smote by lightning, disobedient boys tumble in a tangle down
To drown in the well of others' rage or their own sorrow

Thirst to again return skyward, unbloodied and held close

But to leap is to know the body is the equation the sky has written
And around the body that launches space unfolds its shape of wings

Blue water and blue air are the same substance and within

Now years after he still sings the eerie air along as he walks along the shore
He still knows the secret—that at every moment in the body and breath

One can still plummet and plunge and soar

HYMN

My father's silence I cannot brook. By now he must know I live
      and well.

My heart is nickel, unearthed and sent. We are a manmade
      catastrophe.

Unable to forgive, deeply mine this earthly light that swells
      sickly inside.

Like wind I drift westward and profane when the doors of ice
      slide open.

While he prays my father swallows the sickle moon, its bone-sharp
      path spent.

Preyed upon by calendars of stone unbound the nickel of the mountain
      in streams.

Mine this awful empty night. Mine this unchiming bell,
      his unanswered prayers.

Mine the rain-filled sandals, the road out of town. Like a wind unbound
      this shining river mine—

o

FROM

SILVER

ROAD

o

JANUARY IS A MONTH
WITH TWO FACES

In 1953 Yoko Ono wrote her first score, called *Secret Piece*. It consisted of a musical staff along with two quarter notes under which was handwritten, "with the accompaniment of the birds singing at dawn." To this was later added one line of typescript: "Decide on the one note you want to play. Play to the following accompaniment: The woods from 5 a.m. to 8 a.m. in summer."

I have heard this piece performed by entire orchestras who tromped into the woods to do it, dew-licked and bleary-eyed, and I have heard this piece performed by an individual singer. I have performed this piece myself.

One could talk about it endlessly—how it answers Cage's 4′33″, how it turns the art-maker into the audience and vice versa, and so on—but instead of infinite theoretical meanings here are very practical notions: Firstly, there is a marriage between technology and the body in the combination of typescript and handwriting on the score. Secondly, this kind of art depends not on rules or learning but on the focused perception of any untrained solitary listener. And finally and most importantly, of course, is the fact that the typewritten instructions and the handwritten score beneath it are not the same. Which are you meant to follow? Conceptual art—at least for Ono, one of its progenitors—was not an idea-based mode of taking the artist out of the equation but an occasion for more art-making. By making of the writing an art, she lifted any constraint on "realization" of the music, the painting, the film, etc.

It's worth mentioning that although in the beginning Ono *did* realize her own "instructions," at a certain point she just exhibited the instructions themselves as texts in frames. Now that her work is being shown in retrospectives and one-woman shows, the instructions are again being displayed alongside the realizations, which take the form of recordings, paintings, or objects.

I live in an old house built in 1911. It has not been updated or refurbished. One knows immediately upon entering that one is in an older house with its heavy dark wood doors, fixtures, radiators and built-in bookshelves, hutches, and dressers. You cannot come inside and not feel the temporal remove. The house does not have that blank anonymity of contemporary spaces. Because we bought it from people who'd lived here for fifty years and who'd bought it from the people who built it in 1911, we know its full history. We know what happened to the people who lived in this house.

When I sit on the landing of the staircase which splits in two directions down to the first floor, I know that I hunch down in the same place where the Richards girls hid to listen to the funeral of their father, the house's first owner, which was held in the first floor parlor and which they had been forbidden to attend. When I go up to the yoga practice room on the third floor, I remember that this room used to be one of the dormitories for the students who roomed here in the early part of the century, but that the Schoonmakers who bought the house in 1965 used it as storage space for their camping and hiking equipment.

In this way we are always in context. Charles Olson said he took "the central fact of America to be SPACE," but I think now the central fact of America is ERASURE—erasure of both space and time. In America it is possible to forget which lands belonged to which Indigenous nation. It is possible in America for actually existing Native peoples to protest the use of their lands and still be ignored by the American government.

For a long time I have dreamt of Ono's piece. What is one note I could play at any given moment? Poetry; body practices of yoga, dance, or running; hiking in the mountains; swimming or floating in the ocean; lying on one's back and gazing in the direction of the moon-lonely moon which does not itself illuminate but reveals illumination: these are all practices that allow one—a human body which lives and dies at devastating speed, you will have to agree—to actually see what locality means, how time unravels. You know you are a body that exists in the physical universe, in a context of mass and energy, which do not convert from one to the other but are themselves the same thing.

In the houses of my extended family I sometimes wonder who I am. I am neither professor nor poet nor lover of anyone. My partner's name is known but many of my family have never met him. Our house, that great yellow and blue oasis on the eastern side of Oberlin, Ohio, is unvisited. When I go home for holidays or visits I feel like a spirit somehow, detached from everything, floating through. But time will cruelly divest us of our contexts throughout our lives and we are constantly supposed to invent new ones or see the relationships that once existed in both past and future tenses.

My queerness does not make me a two-spirited person or make available to me any particular magic. It only reveals better that latent quality of loneliness or aloneness shared by any mortal thing. I have come to believe that this sense of alienation is what opened the door for me to poetry.

Time is ordinary, invented and defined by poets and scientists. Every poet, even those who have not studied physics, suspects that time is a fiction, that it is not real, at least not in the way that we think of it. The traditional Persian New Year begins on the first day of spring. The Jewish New Year begins in the autumn, the sunset of the year. The Muslim calendar year is purely lunar and so its beginning floats throughout the year ungoverned by the sun. I prefer this one of course, because it leads the individual into Ono's conundrum: to choose your note, a note that can shift and change throughout the course of one's own life.

Our new year, the American one, the Western one, is the Roman one: devoted to Janus, the god who could look in two directions at once, to the past and to the future. Of course, if time bends then there are a million directions at once and fate is not a line or thread but a tapestry, a web, endless and infinite.

It was Einstein who first imagined that the universe was both finite and infinite. No, that's not correct: that it was finite but *had no borders*. As on the Earth which is round, at the farthest point in the universe one might meet oneself.

Ono's score always contradicts itself—which is the sound meant to accompany the one note played? Neither body nor spirit is absolute concept or actuality. Nothing is. Even considering that, I do not want to forget myself; I do not want to erase the physical in favor of the spirit nor the spirit in favor of the actual world. I want to live in time and space since if in the actual universe there is neither, then this one minute might be my only chance.

You can choose to exist: you can choose not to be a ghost. I learned at a very young age the myth of Abraham and his son, whom God asked him to sacrifice. But I never knew which role was mine to play: that of Isaac the traumatized son ("But father, where is the ram?") or Ishmael the compliant son ("Do what you are commanded father, you will find me steadfast").

There was another myth I dreamed of, all those days as a discontented young man, not yet a poet at all, lingering by the chain-link fence clutching my copy of *d'Aulaires' Book of Greek Myths*, lingering on the story of Ganymede and imagining that of all the youths on Earth, Zeus the King of the Sky would see me and find me most beautiful, that he would soar down not in the shape of a swan or a bull or a god but as a man.

So there I was, a two-faced supplicant, the unwritten son, the one shocked between wolftongue and thunder, eternally alarmed and never ameliorated, committed beyond reason to the actual world yet all the while praying to be abducted curly-locked and fabulous into Heaven.

DRUNK TEXT

in and in between each sway
the cold is hard and solid
I wonder what is it that strays
who loves me even more

which street do I walk on now
how do I take good care
river that hid me or river that drowned
who am I now and where—

ALL WAYS TO KNOW

it is always to change direction always to know

that I quote the sutra-soft orange threads

tying themselves in strings around the cage bars

my bony torso slick with gold squares pressed there

at Sarnath I first heard the syllables of lack

I am 'was'

I was 'want'

want that I lay myself down

smooth on a prayerboard carried forward

the window was broken

the papers were stolen

and I was no where but empty

driven to think myself endlessly forward

at Sarnath a monk tied the string around my wrist

meant to remind me but remind me of what

STAR SAILOR

courage of contrail writing peace in the sky
all my enemies retreat underground

if atlas stumbled and the sky-bell slipped
all the darkness would fall down

we would find ourselves each
stars in space

the whole world blue
and terrified

everyday Cosmonaut
I was so called

Kazim knot
what you told me

not what I claimed
not what stayed with me

naut what I was named

NEWPORT JOURNAL

Walking down the mossy steps to the beach.

Thick green ropes of bullwhip kelp, the kind of seaweed we saw at Point Reyes once, each with its green-ghost head, piles of them everywhere and sometimes a single one calligraphed across the sand.

Swift air, water always rushing three different ways.

Newport at the edge of the continent, ocean here not receding away into depth but dropping immediately.

In Seattle, the pines were so tall, with no low branches, my mind went quickly back to Jenpeg, to my cold cold childhood.

As in Madison, living in water, between lakes, water on three sides.

But Seattle, unlike Newport, protected from endless horizon by the islands. Here you only look and look.

Portland on the river, driving through at night, ablaze with lights.

I thought, turning off the highway from Portland to drive to Newport, on the shore, I would be trapped in the rainy night forever.

Coming through the last stand of trees into town I was shocked to find the town, big, dirty, grittier than Beacon, plainer than Shippensburg, a fishing town without fishing anymore.

Only last week, as five different people told me on the same day, a couple had been swept from the jetty out to sea.

While I walked I thought: I love it, this, walking along the edge of the sea. The sea without end.

Everything without end. Marguerite Duras gave it to me: other languages, a softer sense, other ways of knowing through the sea.

Language without knowing, without sound, without sense. *Sans cesse.*

Now sitting in a warm restaurant, drinking spicy coconut soup and reading poetry by Larry Eigner and Jean Valentine.

Lost always in loss.

I want to look at my hands. I want to say something in the language of the ocean, the language of the rain.

Hurrying back to the hotel I forewent my chance to see the second lighthouse, the more famous one at the northern end of town.

Tonight I go to the art gallery overlooking the ocean to read poems. I drink coffee and dream about transforming.

After the reading the people are very friendly and excited but then leave one by one. I invite my co-reader to have dinner but she is meeting friends and so I am left in the middle of the parking lot, alone, cold and getting colder.

I walk a little bit down the block. There is a man coming the other way walking a little dog. There is a café down the street that serves vegetarian food and hot drinks, he says.

La mer sans cesse.

I hurry down the road. I miss my father.

BAGGAGE CLAIM

maybe I am   a suitcase unspoken for   a seed
inside the sealed seem   stitched between breath and body

me and my   dreaming mind   reaching for
the blue canvas case   conveyed out of grasp

memory of my mother   memory of   all that disappears
in the endless vision overhead   of waves

a plane crashing into water   a suitcase washed ashore
what am I made of   water   am I made of   fire

and my mother is still dreaming   trying to remember
where is my claim check   what is my name

THIRD PERSON

In November—before we've left for South America—my sister enters
the hospital for a stem-cell transplant treatment. This has long been
used to treat leukemia patients but she is in a trial treatment for her
Multiple Sclerosis. It is possible that the new stem cells will regenerate
her immune system and halt the progress of her MS symptoms or even
reverse some of the damage.

No one will be able to tell until the cells are drawn, her immune system
eradicated by chemotherapy, the cells treated and swirled and reinserted
into her.

Since I am on leave from teaching, I am the one most available to go and
stay with her in isolation, where I spend weeks scrubbing, disinfecting,
cleaning, cooking. During the days we occupy the time by watching
endless episodes of *Little House on the Prairie*. In the evenings I go out
and wander the streets of Chicago just to remind myself that I am
someone else besides a caregiver.

Though at the same time it feels incredible to be a caregiver, to give my
whole own identity over to someone else. And to be someone in my
family, not just the middle child, the gay son who is assumed to not care
anything about his parents' wishes, about the culture he came from, the
religion he was raised in.

The prodigal son tenderly takes his sister to have all her hair cut off
because she knows she will lose it anyhow. The son runs interference
with doctors, nurses, with well-meaning relatives who want to visit.
He thinks the sister never even knows how he shepherds people in and
out, helps his mother to "decide" not to come on the days the sister is
run down to the bone, how he subtly encourages another relative whom
she hasn't heard from in a while to call on the day the sister is feeling
especially down.

Months later he will find out that the sister knew—despite the brother's every effort—she knew all along the tricks he was playing on everyone.

She has been sick for decades. After the operations, after the weeks of chemotherapy and the convalescence, she goes home to Florida, and the brother boards a plane for Toronto—for the funeral of their Aunty Najma—and then another plane to South America—to visit his other family, the family of his partner, the family that no one in his first family has ever met.

So I go with Marco south to the mountains, but I keep remembering the time with my sister, how I took the phone or the remote control whenever she needed to use them and gave them each a quick spray and a swipe, the time I spent on hold with the airline changing my tickets when I learned of my aunt's passing.

And that is why and how one moves from first person to third person and back.

DOME OF THE ROCK

It's never been there
What you believe

Ocean or mountain
Who could choose

What heaven clamors for
No one counts on

Three times zero is
The old way home

A CARTOGRAPHY

Sketching the outlines of something
Or knowing by heart how far one travels
How far did I travel to Haifa or to the sea
When I drove with Rachel from the mountains
How do we know how long history will echo

For example the mosque on the road
We didn't know which war it was destroyed in
Or if by mere neglect one side leant dangerously down
Inside covered in graffiti in four languages
The mihrab blackened by fire

No less holy since its primary purpose is to mark direction
In an otherwise empty building
One corner of the room completely exposed to the fields
And across the street a dead cow lying on its side
Three ropes hang down from the minaret

Where some Hasidic boys had scaled the side
And sat on the balcony—what were they doing?
Eating sandwiches, saying their prayers or listening
To the language of the land, the abandoned building or
That carcass lying limp on the side of the road

LARAMIE JOURNAL

Rocks bright yellow, thirty feet high and we walk small between them.

Sapphire sky and glowing white on the ground, rock-bones, rock-bed, rock wonder.

I climb frightful inside the house of stone and spell myself.

In fragmented space and time one sees oneself in slivers and snatches.

Labors of Psyche in ordinary time I climb up on the rock-trails but wanting only the flat ground, the field.

Field of snow, sanctified Matthew, Shepard of everybody.

Every body lashed to the fence, latched to spirit slowly draining from the body in two clear tracks.

What I said to the Missouri students about "mountain time": how is it that mountains in fact mark time.

Clattering in my mind as the snow comes down, I lose myself, lose everything.

Matthias and Julia come, and Eula and Anna, I don't feel alone for the moment.

November in the ground in Laramie snow.

Small book of sentences and theory is bliss because it is the mind wondering about the word or world behind the world or word.

Half of anything (but loneliness) and you are in negative quantity and left.

Left with nothing, all these years and death between us, Janis Joplin still wailing away on the radio.

Why so haunted by ghosts or ghosts of an idea.

Because half loneliness and you are still left there with half and besides lonely for your loneliness.

We trudge through November snow to reach actually nowhere.

Fence gone and emptiness gone: housing developments on two sides and a superstore and parking lot on the third.

Fourth stretches away and away into half loneliness, disappeared death.

Actually nowhere marked.

And take it, take another little piece of my heart.

THEFT

Bicycle missing from the shed in the night
On the screen porch no wind moves through

The orange tabby cat wants to chew through the string
Tied on my wrist meant to remind me

Maybe the bicycle was not stolen but ridden and forgotten
Oh the thief of strings creeps orange through the night

Whispering his hot breath wet in my ear in my mouth
Nibbling away at what holds me

MY CHEWED BOOK

After forty days god blows a spirit into the clot says the Qur'an
And after forty more days it comes to look like a chewed morsel

There is an Antarctic opening in the spine of the sky
I have no ambition for the structure of sign any more

Dream got traced on leaves tied to the sky
I'm tied forward to launch

A baby plucked a book from my hand once
And put it spine first in his mouth to chew

MY LIFE STRANDS

after Zhang Chun Hong

Blocks of pink stone mean it is an Arab house.

Against the ruckled bark of the oak the deep lines in my face are photographed.

At sunrise I walk along the beach as the sky turns the sharpest pink.

Stone stairs lead to the temple in which women are not permitted.

On the way home my scooter skids on all the fallen leaves and I fall.

A poet tells me she is trying to list a hundred different words for stone.

In order to defeat the rampaging demon, Vishnu took the form of Mohini the Enchantress to trick Shiva into giving her a child.

I dress now only in colors of spring: new leaves, first crocus, cherry blossom.

At the foot of the temple stairs a woman named Saraswati looks up.

The figure does not dare breathe but is himself breathed.

Stone is a rain or a river, inseparable.

We bring bunches of forsythia branches inside to force them to bloom.

Nightly as I climb the stone stairs to my apartment, I pass the banana flower.

Your body trembles between incarcerations.

The church is demolished but its basement is still there buried.

Last night someone said, "Palestine goes with you."

Flying over Karachi, I think "My father is down there somewhere."

I turn in no direction but loss, the sun magnet pulling me skyward.

Once seven temples ranged along the shore; six still submerged.

Saraswati begins to climb the eighteen sacred steps to the temple.

Wind steals into me.

How lonely I am among rocks a billion years old.

I was dragged to the olive tree, scent of thyme and pepper in the air.

Snow in the air makes actual sound.

Bodies are violent and vile and refuse to submit.

I drift apart like a garlanded goddess set adrift on the river.

The aspens creak like a ship at sea.

Winds in the aspens like voices steal into me.

The next day Saraswati, released without criminal charges, watches the priests purify the altar.

Oh mountain time send me on.

Sad as a cinder I weep like a stone.

GLACIER

When we stood at the glacier, I was captivated by the colors—a very dark blue, a very bright white.

With crampons strapped to our shoes we negotiated the edges of the glacier, climbing along ridges and smooth valleys. We came to a promontory looking out over the wide landscape of the frozen river. Because of all the melting and refreezing, the top of the glacier is contoured like a mountain range in miniature, complete with peaks and valleys, deep blue crevasses and soaring pinnacles. For a moment it is like I am still in Uttarakhand, staring out at the sun rising over the Himalayas.

Through the valleys and peaks of the constantly forming and reforming glacier, we hear creaks and giant cracks as far beneath the surface the ice shifts and changes position.

Every part of this glacier is every other part, I realized.

Every time and place exists inside one human body.

All light in the world exists at the instant of its own creation.

You are neither mud of the earth nor matter of a star.

You are this silver road advancing, you are the man climbing aloft upon it.

You are a myth, you are music, you are a meeting place.

o

FROM

INQUISITION

o

MAY

And so it came my last day in the sunset, fog sluicing over me.

I turn east in the gaunt dawn and sue the blue dizzy.

At least in the unloving years I had my difference to wield.

THE EARTHQUAKE DAYS

In the earthquake days I could not hear you over the din or it might have
    been
the dinner bell but that's odd
because I'm usually the one
cooking up if not dinner then
a plan to build new fault lines through the dangerous valley

I can't give you an answer right now because I'm late for my
    resurrection,
the one where I step into my angel offices and fuck
the sun delirious
That eclipse last week? Because of me
You're welcome

The postman rattles up with your counteroffer and I'm off
to a yoga class avoiding your call yes like the plague
because son you can read
in the dark and I have no
hiding place left

We walk hand in hand down the hill
into the Castro
avoiding the nudist protest not because we are afraid but
because we already know all about this city, its engineered foundations,
its earthquake-proofed buildings, the sea walls

No tempest will catch us unaware
while we claim our share of
the province of penumbral affections—
You have no reason
to trust me but I swear I lie

down in this metal box as it thunders and looks
inside my brain. I am terrified nothing
is wrong because otherwise
how will I rewrite the maps unmoored
a deep sea a moor a cosmonaut

Who needs saving more
than the one who forgot
how the lazy cartographer mislabeled
his birthplace as Loss?
Riding the bus out to the end of the lines and back

I collect trash for art, oil spill, spent forest, the mind
is at work and everything is at stake—I demand
statehood for my states of mind, senators
for my failure, my disappointment, the slander
and my brain unmapped reveals no

explanation for danger the ground untamed
I make paintings of nothing and
stand before them like mirrors
I only recently became a man but I do
not want to let go of my boy-weakness

instead I want to meet God in heaven and in long psychotropic odes
have Him send me again digging in the dirt to unleash
tantric animal governors to lay down
the orgasmic law twice skewered and miserable
in the old photographs, miserable in my body, huddled

next to my mother, recently permed and aglow so unaware
of what is about to hit her—that I am the answer to Bhanu's question:
"Who is responsible for the suffering of your mother?" and so sick
I considered that sickness
could bring us closer and Shahid and Allen in heaven

shake me by the shoulders three times because they want me
to know that this world is worth its
trembling. At the next table over a mother
tries to reconcile her bickering sons
I have no brother but the one

I invent has always got my back, he drowns
out the mullahs so my mother can finally hear me
In a different book Jesus
never suffered, never was flogged or died
went whole into heaven without passion

Shall I then deny myself passport through the stark places
unsalvageable, imagine it, the Mother
of Sorrows did never grieve in the new season
trees smell of semen and the tectonic plates
make their latest explosive move:

to transubstantiate my claim
by unraveling this city down to stone
Everyone I know wants to douse
the fire, flee the endless aftershocks,
untangle every vexing question

You owe me this witness

I owe you flames

FLOWER GATE

Edged in petals I affix myself to the gate
at every appointed prayer hour

Seed pods scatter in silver dusk
Green cypresses minaret the sky

My disobedient body aspires and I
when music pierces inland hand in hand

devour this arbor of forgetting
and take one last shot at sharing your fiery fate

In the end I am not you
Not a garden nor a gate

But just a scruffy hustler, willing to hop the fence
and spend himself bare to nothing

ABU NUWAS

Halfway between the northern and southern sky

Hangs the constellation of Abu Nuwas

Who drunk and in love knelt at places rivers split

To refuse all paths and offer his mosaic prayer

Unhinged he peeled from yellow-leafed birches enough paper

To fashion a barque and make for the moon

Floating in the moment where one wave becomes another

Amber driftwood or beach glass or lost unmapped stars reciting

We are what produces itself sanded and cast adrift

Precisely at the horizon and so eternally unseen

One note emerges from the drizzle of sound

What finally somehow though endless does wash ashore

JOHN

Who was I when I was writing this name

Copper oxidizes to green

Air packs itself tight in the seed

Seed unspools in the ground writing the biography of dirt

A little down the road another tower is going up

A man holds his briefcase over his head like an umbrella

In the rain bodies are soft and disappear into sound

On John Street almost choking on loneliness

And the waters of the river nothing so much as the air around us and ash

What would outlive us drifts sparkling into the October air

When you ask who am I past this storm-tossed vessel

The one you're always bailing out

It is just another way to ignore this constant unraveling

This always reaching for an end when clearly there's no end in sight

HIS MOSAIC PRAYER

Trial by magnolia
You never understand

Sane and unchanged
Strip down to rain

Cross examined by
Northern lights

My wont was to know you
Uncovered cup of sulfured sun

Struck my bell of breath
Unreachable this ruin of effort

Muttered perfumed profanity
Unsolvable these equations

Unanswerable these letters
Of despair this air that errs

ORIGIN STORY

Someone always asks me "where are you from"
And I want to say a body is a body of matter flung
From all corners of the universe and I am a patriot
Of breath of sin of the endless clamor out the window
But what I say is I am from nowhere
Which is also a convenience a kind of lie

When I was sitting in the Mumbai airport this January
On a forty-hour layover rushing home because
My mother had had a stroke and was not yet verbal
I wondered about my words
Perhaps I am from my words
Because the basic biography is ordinary

Born in Croydon to a mother and a father who
On different sides of a national border
Were married in wartime and had to reunite in England
The only place they could both get to
Born at home—76 Bingham Street
Midwived and not doctored into the world

Taken back to India when the war was over
Where I came into language and of the seven
That were spoken in the house I began speaking four as the same
Then to the cold Canadian north we went to a town that no longer exists
On the other side of Cross Lake from the People
Who lost everything because of the dam my father was helping to build

Then to Winnipeg then to New York City
Then to Buffalo
Which I can claim
I can say I am from Buffalo because

It is a city of poets
The city of Lucille Clifton

I arrive there in cold January to find my mother
A little slowed down but still self-possessed enough
To cook meals for everyone
Even if she didn't remember the names for all the spices she was using
She talks by the time I arrive but slowly and deliberately
And she has to listen very carefully to be able to respond

She pauses while she talks and cocks her head while she thinks
She does not criticize me nor say anything about my wild hair
Our ordinary silence does not seem as suffocating
Because I wait patiently while she strains to find each word
And what on earth does it mean that
I almost like my mother better this way

When she goes to her medical appointment
I get out my copy of *good woman* and comb through its lines
To find the addresses where Lucille Clifton lived
I climb into the car with a map and a journal and drive
Through the snow to find those places and take photographs
Of the empty lots where the houses once stood

Listen:
I have no answer to your question
I am not kidding when I tell you:

I earned my own voice
The shape it makes in the world holds me
I have no hometown no mother tongue

I have not been a good son

SARASWATI PUJA

On the water in the morning dark shapes emerge

Sewn on the surface of god and ardor:

History a hysterical marigold bloom,

Oarsman pulling with beautiful rhythm,

his eyes covered by dark glasses

Dismembered reed arms float past, Saraswati comes apart

His oar dips in, crushing the floating marigolds

At the Jain ghat a huge painted swastika,

symbol unmoored from meaning

I want him to take off his glasses, to look at me

Open his orange lips, flower-stained and speak to me

What do we have to do to own our life

Water has no architecture in warm places

It will not stay where it is spilled

THE FAILURE OF NAVIGATION
IN THE VALLEY

to C.D. Wright

No body is fixed in position no one can be known

Still I am read by satellites my tendencies extrapolated

In the mountains I have no GPS I don't know where to go

There are those trees their leaves flicker like little jewels a whole bucketful

Darkness stares back are you even human anymore

I close the curtains at night not because I think others will see in

Turn left there but so I do not see the reflection that is pure dark

I am not afraid of anything (oh is that so)

Citizen bear do this place not belong to you

Unseen I wander through the thorny place of what I (no that ain't it)

No fear can be knew can be none fuck how do you spell it

I held a heavy jade pendant in my hand once not in this valley in another

In the range of limited human experience how many places are there really

I don't even have to look at the earth anymore I just have to listen

Now that hillbilly whisper guides me which way to turn how far up the turn is

Drawling like moonshine we're really off the grid now

Making wild prayers to the green dark (I love this kind) (which kind do you mean

Moonshine grid prayers or night) does it matter (it matters)

(Thank god we thought of having her record this voice) I mean every kind

TRICK

Your life among cinematic disasters: tidal wave, swamp thing, tsunami

A wickedly souped-up bore just minutes before the lights go on

Doubly pathetic because daylight saving offered you an extra empty hour

You count your body up in coins and curses and think:

There must be another body inside me, tougher, sunnier, more beautiful

If only I could fuck him free

And the one you want, the dirty blond with the filthy mouth
and pierced tongue is long gone and you are what you've always been:

A squirrelly punk, dizzy with gin, losing your shirt, climbing into the cage

LETTER TO ZEPHYR FROM
THE ONCE-BOY HYACINTH

Unhook each point from the silver-backed sky.
Unfasten the buttons of my winter jacket and petal me.

Dear fickle once-a-year wonder, reach for me even now, will you,
but know my stem wanders lightward even as your gusts thrust
through the soil into me. Rage in your comely way but know
you arrived every year on his heels, that yellow timeless fire-starter
who shone madly on me even in the cold months. Perhaps I lack
vision, lying with the wonder that arrived first but I thought only
to master my mother's ken. Take comfort at least that I know
it was your roughness that invented me, made beautiful my ruin.

More than merely warm me, you murdered me into music.
You killed my fearful youth and brought me to flower.

THE LABORS OF PSYCHE

Sail or spin I endless ember

In the house of flowers am undone

My crime comes in hot slicks

Plunder now each crushed night

Skylight open wide to snow

Very coldly thrust through

Look now at each unmapped surface

Very hungry spun smooth

Who in the dark comes to pounce

Drinking heat straight from the bottle

My mouth deeply tongued and

By swollen bud's dehiscence opened

You lie on top of me in this siren cave

Breathing whirl of duende innuendo

Come now together between anarchy and will

Bright pharo of flower throat

My fortune lines do still bewilder

Eternal spring now pistil thin

You spin me psychophonic to corolla harbor

Nocturne thrust you exhale I sunder

PERSEPHONE AS A BOY

His father used to say, "Your face is like a flower."

At seven each morning he wakes with the sun, imagines it burning
through the window. He dreams he has cancer burning through his skin
but has never been to a doctor.

Yesterday he imagined a death even better, spectacular and violent:
Crazy taxi, stray bullet, runaway train—

In the final scene of this film he's lying there with wide eyes,
mouth trembling, struggling to speak to his father,

who is for some reason in New York with him,
holding his hand and saying his scripted lines,
"Don't try to say anything. I love you."

At seven forty-five he throws back the covers,
puts a jacket on over his pajamas and walks to the corner store
for small things he doesn't need, just to remind himself he is alive:
daisies, pomegranates, green tea, salt.

Passing the subway stairs on his way home he realizes
he could go underground here and, by ticket and transfer,
not emerge again from the earth for hundreds of miles.

DRONE

Do strangers make you human

Science fiction visiting bodies as cold fact

What unknown numbers govern our genes or phones

A constant thrum from outer space

Snow makes a sound in sand

You are seen from far above

Will the myth explain you

Unheard and vanished

Bodies dismember to dirt

Hardly alive, hardly a person anymore

Who will I be next and in that life will you know me

THE DRESSMAKER OF GALILEE

He wears himself down wild uncertain,
laps the frayed thread-end
with his clumsy tongue.

He wants to know as well what the body
and its coverings could teach him about
genders of flesh.

The Druze have a secret book.
Some know what's in it,
some don't. No one minds.

His voice falls to pieces when he claims
for himself the spaces
of flowers or silk.

At the worried seam of the border between
what is taught and what is felt, some Druze know
we are all about to switch genders.

With eyes the same silver as his tailor's needle,
in the globe of barbarous heat
he stakes his claim stitch by stich.

He never learned how to behave.
He knows only he must sew one piece to another
and spike heaven sense

MARIE'S CRISIS

We stumble through the strafing night to any harbor we think safe
and we find one on some corner in the West Village called Marie's Crisis
and in it scores of men huddle around a grand piano and sing songs
together. At some point, a woman who looks like Helen Terry,
the big backup singer from Culture Club, emerges from the kitchen
to sing a number for the boys.

The crowd falls silent and she starts belting it out and immediately
I want to know *wait what is the crisis?* And immediately after *why
is a song called a "number"?* I know Pythagoras believed that music
resonated between planets and that the notes of the scale could be
calculated, that each note itself was not even singular
but had a dominant tone with seventeen other harmonic tones underneath.

Or am I making all this up? And why do you care?
And why haven't you taken your pants off yet?
Marie is singing Janis Joplin and I imagine that I can actually feel
the porosity of the table under my fingers. There's a cute skinny blond
at the bar. He's wearing a short-sleeved plaid shirt which I think
I can get on board with but ironed jeans with boat shoes, not so much.

I'm trying to figure out exactly what to say to him but my field is
physics not chemistry. I open with "I wrote my dissertation
on the agitation that occurs in worldsheets during a redshift event."
Not my strongest effort. He responds with, "In Indian dance, the face
is actually an instrument of the body and so its expressions
are part of the choreography."

Marie looks like she's about to burst out laughing. I know the look,
it's called "show-tune face." Look ridiculously happy while belting out
whatever song at hand at the top of your lungs. No one cares, she's singing
Sinatra.

I met a kid in Brooklyn once who said he was Frank's son: he grew up
with his mom in suburban Jersey and Frank never acknowledged him
but used to come around and have dinner with them every once in a while.

It was the night my friend Ava taught me how to take tequila shots
and I had seven and ended the night chatting up Danny
in between his stints dancing on the bar.
I found I didn't really have anything to say to him except
that I believed him, that I thought Frank really was his father,
that he looked just like him.

As soon as I'd said it "These Boots Are Made for Walking"
came on the radio and I thought it pretty likely that was a sign
but I didn't say anything and I don't know what Danny was thinking
because he didn't say anything either. Marie is singing a bluesy,
folksy version of "I Saw the Sign" and it makes me remember
my friend Araki who used to be my lover and then only my friend

but maybe isn't even that anymore because I haven't heard from him
in eight months and I have no idea what he is doing, because
all he ever posts on Facebook are links to news stories about public health.
Marie's voice is scratchy and smoky and whiskey-soaked.
It's not even what you'd call pretty or good but she is singing
for everything she's worth. The bar is cute but small and a little shabby,

and the blond wants to know if I'll sing a duet with him
when Marie is done and that makes me think either I better
marry him or make a run for it while I've still got some lead time.
I can't sing but I have developed an equation that can calculate exactly
how long it is going to take for you to take off your pants.
Don't say physics doesn't have any practical applications.

Then someone tells me that's not even Marie, it's Maggie the night manager.
It's been a week since that club in Florida got shot up and my parents
have yet to call to see how I'm doing. Maggie is singing the Boy George part

of "Church of the Poison Mind" and I'm three sheets to the wind anyhow
so I'll tell you what I'm going to do, I'm going to climb up on top
of that piano and do the Helen Terry part.

Maggie's voice is straining and it's not even her crisis.
She's the biggest star in the room and a girl needs backup.

YANNIS RITSOS

Athens was welcoming to those who had come from the sea.
MAHMOUD DARWISH

Yannis, you held him in the glare of the diamonded sea,
unteaching him his practical mantra of liberation,
maybe seeing in him a son to take care of you in your loneliness,
loneliness varnished by your detention

in the house made of flower stems that thrust
through the rocks in the prison-yard, its roof made
of unscannable lines of rain. You revealed to him
the sound of the rusty-hinged door, how it would swing

sadly open and reveal no homeland beyond at all.
He came from the sea dragging his anklets of keys.
Did you teach him then how the old locks and houses
of his hometown were already all broken?

Yannis, in the end he rinsed the last of the coast road's
dust from his body after a lifetime of pressing his language
into lines of poetry and prayer and prestidigitation,
tired of praising mosques in which he could not pray.

The same morning I was forbidden by the guard to pray
at the Mezquita of Córdoba, he woke up in Houston,
Texas and went to a mall food court to meet for the first and last time
his translator. The words they spoke to one another

were the same as those I saw in stone fragments
on the floor of the archeological dig at Madinat al-Zahra,
the ruined capital of the West looking East toward
the cities left behind. That city had remained buried

in a field for a thousand years. The palace and throne room
had been torn apart, the rubble of the mosaics
now being painstakingly reassembled piece by piece,
unlike the villages of Palestine, disassembled down to stone.

Yannis, what did you say to him that blue afternoon when the stone
canoe landed and he arrived in another place that would be home and
not-home? In Córdoba, meanwhile, the story of his death flashed
across the morning news, scrolling along the screen from clay to nothing.

But let's let the sea have the last word, the sea he crossed to come
to you, or the one that sparkled off the coast of Chile when he,
in Neruda's house, remembered you or the sea that rained
lightly down as the poet and his translator huddled together

over cheap food-court coffee to converse, in a shopping mall in Texas,
though it could have been Athens, or Palestine, or Neruda's house,
at least as good as any mosque in the world,
so long as there was coffee and poetry and the sound of rain,

rain in the shape of the river, rain in the shape of a broken lock,
rain in the shape of long-since written verses, while the translator
of lost homelands makes from the sound of butterfly wings
rain in the shape of the dark furnace of days.

RANDOM SEARCH

Who will in the night unpetaling lose himself in fealty
His crime heartbreaking, confessed and festering
What undresses in the ground, lost in perjury

He's to be tried for the nearly unforgivable sins of naming
Ordinary stars after himself, drinking coffee without labor laws
Marking time by the icicle melting from the eave

Chaste and chastened, he is touched by you
His body changes as he sinks under your hands
The world's opulent answer, his silent umbrage

A submerged body arrows to the surface
Not by intent but because it is buoyant
He wants to save you, wants to save everyone

Hand him back his glasses and he tells you to
Renounce meat and demand an end to inheritance
And then he's off to recite Arabic in the gate area

What else is left but to be human here

TEXT CLOUD ANTHOLOGY

Afternoon alive angel Ali
Belted by birds
Blue boat of your body
Breaks in breath
Broken brother come in
Dark disappear down
Don't exist
The empty editor echoes
Eternal fast find me forgotten
The garden glass hasn't heard yet
To hollow its horizon higher
Inside Kazim
Kazim knew
Learned light
Listened
Lived lost
Limited himself to matter
His memoir of morning
Mother mountain mouth
Never night this orifice open
Orating to ovation
Plucked pot pieces of plot
His prayer pulled quickly from rain
Recitation of rain rejoining the rocks
Rocks rushed to remembering the secret series
Of sun wonders, silence on the shore
Silence someone sounds
Speaking through stone
The sunset stringing us along
Students of the task that of thirst
A thousand trees to teach this trick to us
To understand the voice the verse the version of vanishing

That waits and wants and wonders
Wheel window wander
Yesterday you yearned in the yews
You know then who you were
Who you gathered yourself to be
Zamindar of zinnias
Zephyr through the zoo

ALL ONE'S BLUE

One must—like God—spend all one's blue
AGHA SHAHID ALI

In the empty rooms of sky I lingered
For a year and a day only now
Do I wonder in which blue vestment
Dawn will I don in thunder raiment
Rains and send this letter to far
Gods who knew nothing of how
A room by cloud and atom warm
Could add to a human body the share
That birds have to roam no room
Then clear to the horizon mark a vertical
Creature bear I earthbound and clever
Beyond measure do swear oblivion
Has its own markers but where the buoy
Of being clangs its stellar ore

APASMARA CLIMBS TO
THE MOUNTAIN LAKE

First at the shore the water so blue it disappears into the afternoon of
   my eye
I am marked by flowers, my body a boat that seeks to cross the wide reach
   of it
Abandoned by those who accompanied me
My old fear of depths returns and I wonder
How long divided by valley and springfall will I be allowed to stay
Here, ungoverned but thrilled by light and salt I turn up the rock-trail
   to seek
The long-lauded gorge all the others were permitted to climb to long ago

As I hop the stile to follow, I look back
To the beach and see small figures moving
Was that how I too was seen? Having never thought to climb before
The matter feels not unimportant but irrelevant. After all, the shape
One's body makes in the ocean cannot be mapped
But here on the trail I hold close all my failures:
That I am always afraid of being unloved
That I am the stupidest person I know
That I do not call my mother
That I forgot my sunscreen

There's always in the back of my mind the blue blank of my old hometown,
Long since claimed back into the Canadian wilderness
And all the hometowns before and after that I never claimed, never found a
   home in.

The current of the world buffets us, we cannot be still, the deeper we go,
   the calmer

But I always stay here where the breath of the depths
Comes in and the undertow wants to drag me back out

The well of the deep *wants* us
The deep life—sex, god, death—it *wants* us

Land, like the body, has a shape that can be seen and known but what
    I know
About my own body is almost all wrong
It's a flowering plum that decorates my arm in bright pink, not a cherry like
    everyone always tries to sell me on

Can I be entered
Can the ocean make me
Can the flower know me

I am already written down in gunfire and criminal code
The seeds of next year already in the ground, remember
The phenomenal sun unfurls
A million geological years shift the rocks of the trail up
Above the surface of the water
These rain patterns
These subvolcanic seismic shifts
These plants and birds yield to the history of an island forming anew

Neither map nor molecule I am battered
Fractal coastline extrapolated from patterns of moss on a tree
Or the electron's sonic path

Yes I know—"sonic" is wrong
I'm no scientist but I have a song
It vibrates neither in seven tones nor twelve but in all the space between
Usually thought of only as a whine or hum

Water tumbles now from the ridge into the icy mountain lake
Tumbles not without pattern but in fulfillment of Shiva's dance,
Entropy which is chaos of order unspeakable

I heard the painter of waterfalls once say she does not utilize craft or
    technique but rather makes decisions and so perhaps god is a little bit
    like that

Low as a lawman, god chooses colors and canvases
And then the day like paint poured from the top and allowed to fall
    uncommanded

Beacon spree of bullets can light any dark

My mother's voice allowed through the pulse of world-noise

Still, supposedly the universe wields its laws
A body must fall
Water may not stay in the same state
Rain follows physics
Opera sonnets song box to the quantum point of et cetera

Lookit: Chance, Liquid and Gravity are hardly the type of gods a boy would
    put much faith in but in my case those were the only ones who would
    accept me into their worship

They said:
Light every candle
Cross your fingers
Stake your claim to being the dumbest thing that ever lived
Oh but wow I should be so lucky because unless I can release every line
    inked
How will the new ocean ever be able to enter and know me

I'm no beautiful thing
Most days I can hardly stand up straight and breathe
My whole time in the earth has ground down to this degradation:
That even this poor unloved body, these stark days
Even abandoned I seek height
Even while you are opening and entering me, killing me,
I am too much a brute to get the hint

Water screams down from the ridge into the gorge
Equations scatter in a spangle of flower light
Ground down into ignorance and death
My cheek against the sticky rock
God's foot between my shoulder blades
Pressing all the air out of me
My blood freezing in the shock of mountain pool
Burning in shame for not being able to muscle up and rise
Crushed by every element ever invented
Yet I will not relinquish this ignorant ugly shape
I rage I snarl
I want
This life

o

THE
VOICE OF
SHEILA
CHANDRA

o

HESPERINE FOR DAVID BERGER

Begin with the dining room attendant at the ivy-covered university who smashed the stained-glass window because we are now actually going to change history

Imagine then in the suburbs of Cleveland a sculpture of steel rings broken in halves but opening up away from the bullet-written history of the burning helicopter toward the open sky

Seems possible because there is a bridge between general relativity and quantum mechanics that no physicist has yet ascertained

Imagine neither a conditional future if the past were different nor forging ahead from the broken but something newer that bridged that loss

For example what if a painter left the canvas entirely and instead looked at all the extant surfaces in the already man-made and man-frayed world

History then as fragile as stained glass and yet writing new narratives that shape every movement forward

Both ways of understanding the behavior of matter cannot be true yet somehow they still behave as true on the lived-in planet

David Berger at 27 deciding to move across the world to Israel to train and compete in the Olympics 1972 Munich

What Corey Menafee did is he climbed up on top of a table in the dining room and with the long handle of his broom he

Sang in bits and pieces to god the road you knew which was the confusion road the one made of all your wrong turns

Geometry of a building makes it stand math is mighty there are abstractions in every letter their architecture makes sound possible

For each of you a practice Qur'an 5:48 says if God had willed He would have just made you one people

Imran Qureshi does not paint on canvases but paints little blossoms on the ground on the wall in corners of the room they bloom like water or blood or light

While the Qawwali singer Amjad Sabri groans his throat open in ecstatic sound aiming to reach from the muck of the earth all the way into heaven

From the summit I plummet then into the time of unstrung lyres to try to go back into the dark time

A letter arriving in the night-mysterious reads *A reminder we do not forget we do not forgive*

Translator of frozen scripts you try to tongue your way through
that old score shame that I am still trying to settle

Sky boat bear me down along these reticent cords while I plumb
lupine fields in search of lingering snow

Do you know what your body is do you know what god is

Music that do sound off strings into voice from the body's drum
that sings breathe through as wind

Shattered the panes of the stained-glass window depicting
enslaved workers bearing cotton along a road

Hesperus the evening star shines with a cold light through the
tightest drawn evenings sharp-edged and dissolute

He said he didn't even think about it he came into work in the
dining room everyday and he hated that one image in the glass and one
day he just

And of all that was wrong was a pattern painted not last year or
a hundred years ago but I mean yesterday or this morning

Sun is going down on the wrong horizon the sea glows green
then blue then green again this is where I was born this in-between
place

And so I curse the fucking dawn that grinds men to powder
tears them from their bodies flings them down the hot dark barrel of a
gun

How then to catalog the metadata of all the corpses that locate
for us our own bodies and register their Western comfort

Bullet punching through a body like punching through a ticket
registering it for passage

Do you know what god is what's not do you know what art is
what's not do you know what a nation is a citizen a crime

Sir this world has always asked me for my labor then been silent
upon delivery

Star of evening's twin brother was Phosphorus star of morning
who rose up in the dawn and brought new day metaphor of course for
new life

Savage spill and splendid this tended plot a plant this polity
close to alarm smoke in the hallway the door opening the key stolen
shadows appearing

What is the sound of misdemeanors hefting the minutes like
prison tattoos when they took David Berger and his roommates and then
five others in the second apartment sought

I crunch down in the room of my life to draw small blossoms in
the corners of the world flowers or water or light what do I have against
the intention of violence but these small chromatic gestures nothing

While I pretend the sound I howl has some direction this
impossible world always a gate opening could be the death of me

What passes from beyond the horizon of the black hole can
define how the universe is made because if we are right we are right but

The window shattered and glass rained down onto the street
outside the custodial worker was arrested but the university declined to
press the charges

The beautiful were made beautiful the blood in their bodies
sang and in the rain of white phosphorus into the streets of Gaza

This technique of Qawwali depends on the old belief that God is
found in abstraction and in sound say the Sufi teachers it is the physical
matter of the universe made

Theoretical physicist Stephon Alexander then plays a Coltrane
riff and reveals its score which maps a shape that corresponds to the
equation describing a particle of space-time

You did learn in painting directly on stone or the concrete
sidewalk or the notes nesting in the throat or body against body
wrestling or tumbling in space

Register then my ticket on the train in France the machine says "composter" and in that space between languages I am found

I have come back to this village on the Mediterranean shore after sixteen years who was I then the same age as David Berger same age as Mohammed Al-Khatib

"Compost" as in compost the old tomatoes into the earth make a complete system of the body's history into the future life

Are we then only particles of light and liquid and petaled material swirling one into the other lighthouse dark unlit instrument silent

But then the Greeks learned from the Babylonians that the evening star and the morning star that they had envisioned and made gods of and written poems about were in fact the same heavenly body

I register the old tomatoes back into the earth try to clear the trail of ants on the counter swarming the counter where I sliced them

We live by laws of men drawn of laws of gods men say are real who then erected the frame for this chainsaw night

And at this moment on the sea I see in the water a reflection of every face I've known each wave contains another wave each moment of violence contains

Architecture of the Holocaust Remembrance Center outside Jerusalem based on the Hebrew letter *yud* for memory or remembrance but does it remember the forests around it were the site of the destroyed village Deir Yassin

In either case we are inventing the past which means it changes the future which means the machine of time is real made of gears and parts

Register each body like tickets for the train

Munich 1972 the road leads right through young men's brightest hours no question of a Palestinian team not then not now

Ramallah 2016 Mohammed Al-Khatib laces up his running shoes ridiculously trying to train as a sprinter with neither spikes nor coach nor starting block

Each moment of time is a part of space and each piece of space-time is a physical object an object that can be graphed and mapped

Impossible to see impossible to feel to refract how finished the pattern that is every unfolding

Bright glass of many colors the slaves hauling cotton shattered and flickering down toward the concrete

What am I without these things but no question at all

And yet here is Coltrane mapping the nature of the universe
in sound here is David Berger using his body to show the potential of
strength Mohammed decides by guts and grit he can imagine himself
faster

And so I shout down with ragged throat this encroaching blue
that brings dawn then brightening day then David and his teammates
hustled by the kidnappers into a helicopter bound for the airport
promised passage out of Germany

There is no *fajr* call here on the seaside to alert me to the hour
but I can hear creatures stirring from sleep a gift so like death it reeks

Night resounding with Coltrane's whining instrument his
breath through brass has somehow arrived at the same calculation as

Mohammed seeks to shave tenths of seconds off his time there
is no accounting for the decision of the body toward its sport

He would have made you one people but He wanted to try you, so
strive alongside one another toward good deeds, to God you will all return and
then he will account and explain to you the differences you had

Somehow sound improvised in time creates that geometric
pattern of branches swirling or the equation that tells

At the beginning of the universe Amjad Sabri sings away for all
he's worth his voice unspooling *soie sauvage* like a bolt of raw silk like an
untamed spirit

He hopes to find God echolocate Him deep in the harmonic
overtone perhaps at precisely the place his voice breaks

In the end it don't matter whether blood is particles or rivulets
they spill just the same like Qureshi's painting of little red flowers
rosettes of blood on the floor where the mass shooting took place his
flowers covering the place where blood once marked

Or on walls following blue streams following the sewer pipe or
the slicks of sunlight on the windowpane

This unending pattern of abstraction to say we can inscribe
ourselves into the landscape we can change the past we can write
ourselves as a letter arriving unannounced to god with no return address

What other explanation does any scholar have for the verses
of the Qur'an that are neither sentences nor sayings but mere glyphs of
letters

Alif Lam Mim

Ta Ha

Alif Lam Ra

And physics knows what Sabri is hungry for that the point of
breaking a bullet enters David Berger's left shoulder

Unlike the others he is shot while still in the apartment perhaps
to intimidate the other prisoners or perhaps he tried to resist

Because he saw the lip of the black hole as the possibility to   .
know and it is that which tipped us off that the systems do match

Everything thought was true still behaves as if it is true but both
things cannot in the lived-in universe be actually true

If we are on a continuum a wave where time and space bend
then nothing is supposed to emerge from the event horizon and yet

Corey Menafee climbed up on the table he just said *It's 2016 I
shouldn't have to come to work and see things like that That thing's coming
down today I'm tired of it*

Mohammed left Palestine to go to Houston Texas where he
found enough open space to run and train *I only wanted to hear Palestine's
anthem in the stadium* he said

To hear is to make real

Coltrane was a physicist

Sabri found a way to god

David Berger left his home in Cleveland to move to Israel to lift
weights and compete and so at the end of it when the bodies of the ten
others return to Israel David's body is flown back to the States alone

These boys' bodies are made of particles that travel one into the
other and I curse the crepuscular moment dark and light what are you
what is god what isn't

Not until epochs of time later did the Romans look into the sky
at Phosphorus whose name means Bearer of Light and translate into
their own language as Lucifer

Called also Son of Morning

Does every journey continue down the barrel of a gun from
the Olympic village to the helicopter to the airport where the trick was
played to the shootout to the firestorm

What sound breaks the circle of action and reaction

If space do bend then time

Can history be unwoven the tightness released to make it possible to breathe and write anew

Are we pieces made up of pieces made up of pieces

In little licks like a mother cleaning a baby with her animal tongue Sabri draws red petals into the air in sound

David Berger's body straining to life or Mohammed's body racing

Gray endless stone in the cemetery in the suburb of Cleveland I wandered looking for the grave

Sound emerges the sound of the sea from the blue saxophone notes trickling from Qureshi's paintbrush

Glass littering down the window to the street clear the sun shines through

In the suburbs of Cleveland past the shopping mall through the office park nestled up against the interstate is a pedestal of black steel broken rings

Do you even know at all or do you just have to sing to find the place a voice breaks

There is no tradition in the literature of the world of the
hesperine not a serenade nor an aubade but rather a curse to first
darkness itself begging it not to fall a poem against the falling of night
to ward off death the first mortal death was murder and so all this
geometry may be inevitable a tired rehearsal

The stones I left on David's tomb mark what in the end may
be just my passing that a living person was very briefly here looking to
touch the dead

So do we have to just reach up and shatter it that image of David
and his teammates held at gunpoint in the apartment the police so
anxious to move them from the Olympic Village

Broken circles that approach the sky the way a flower would or a
fountain or a bird

Can we sing over the noise or paint down on the stone once
marked by flesh and death can we move forward without breaking

As Sabri's voice breaks his body breaks he wonders does it
always happen that the divine begins when the mortal is shattered

A gunshot begins the race

Dusk turns then to night turns to dawn then turns to day bodies
infect and inflect each other with particles small moments of light and
dark

Qureshi paints another little red flower down do he pray that history may be erased by beauty

How can one create in painting in sound in the poetry of the body the new and abiding future life

Bodies separated by years and miles and religion and law may release their own energy may transfer into one another may be the same body

Is the reality of the physical universe a continuum of time and space or is it made of moments that can move backward and forward can the past be changed

Hesperus makes a play for the sacred space of grief Phosphorus rains down upon Gaza into the bodies of unmade sprinters weight lifters pole vaulters gymnasts

What if God is improvising like Coltrane

Ta Sin Mim

There's no time left David has a plane to catch says good-bye to his parents

'Ain Sin Qaf

The broomstick shatters the glass window and the image litters down

Kaf Ha Ya 'Ain Suad

A voice then breaks as evening covers us in a downpour what else what else

Ya Sin

End then not in the present moment nor in some deathless wished-for past but somewhere very ordinary a normal day a spring day perhaps a little chilly there is Mohammed in the hills above Ramallah lacing up even though there is no open ground to run no coach to train him no spikes for his shoes no starting blocks

FROM "THE VOICE OF SHEILA CHANDRA"

Breaks is constant was like
The river light on the river
Riven that remained a rift
An old rill that sounded
She merged with the vibe
Ration of the drum a hum a
Home womb and um
She OM moaned in the loam
Dark earth come Sheila
Dame ocean dome this poem
Roam to tome tomb foam
Original fountain that fed
My mom Zam-zam when I
Was born

Long before she lost it drift-
S unanchored wanted to merge
And the body of the singer become
The body of the instrument
Talk to the drum find it hum
Study its vowels she made her vow
To sound slowly syllable by
Syllable she pronounced words
In Uzbek word unmoored word
Pure sound oh river long had I
Been long seasons invaded
By your current devoured your tongue
Of water those years time bent
My one voice spoke

Carried cacophony world wheel
Into the human one small voice
Box pool swum midnight we went
Into the sea expecting our prayers
Might carry themselves across
The silver-slammed surface would
Be answered or do they answer
Pale cut of prayers do not answer
Like back into the dark water what
Are those stripes of light across
The room a shape that evaporates
Upon waking what language cannot
Hold onto what you cannot
Hold onto

How to transcribe what flickers what is not
Fixed that voice letters made not of ink but light
Not words of fire on stone how do you transcribe
The blank vowel all the after that aerates
Not disappear but settle down through air
You do not want to say but sing where might
Be rain be sky come down by snow but know
You invite it to cover you the blanket your coat
A heavy pressure god pressure of rain you want
To start the song over but do not dare to be ready
No tune no cadence nothing to pick up no bridge
To cross now to be small again break through
There is no beginning to any song only the place
The singer picks up the tune

What represses unhomes in the sound
Who has made me what is made me
Is a voice just muscles and shape and
Breath to phrase a song boats assemble
At the mouth of the harbor mouth in
Earth you who wrote an ode to silence
Never wrote of what is silenced I did
Seek all resounding caves let the voice
Be lit all the lanterns in the new world we
Need the language of stone from string
To string quiver in the opening the garden
So beautiful Lucifer dark sun of morning
No Eden but innocence no expulsion
But after

Music spent my breath to achieve or invent
Death each chord or cadence out of
Reach out of tune last time in this town
I promised vow or vowel to turn
My back forever on chaos and give
Myself instead to music organizing
Itself in my ear from chaos a river
Made rather than music that makes
A shape of endless seconds I devoted
Myself to the equation of numbers
Between each sound a formula that
Matches planets and atoms music
Is not an art but science I could have
Remained alive but I broke

No more will I listen to other than
A single note moaned not known
I do not here think again what place
Presents here a body as a battery
Of the one moment to open
Your mouth to plug in I will allow what
I invented to find its color make
A shape which neither water nor
Sky do how do you now in this
Contained shape go through
Your life not like a constellation
Not guessed at intuited or divined
No name so how do you discern a shape for
What is often called god

Sheila Chandra sings without words
Because a word is a form of rage at
Death the implicit formlessness
Of the body which translates as
The soul does not cohere every
Feeling of a body as mortal means
Separately French *mot* and *mort*
What do we know and can't tell
Of the deep black of the world of
Death of the painting on the wall
I in past days trusted border
Zones relinquished homes sounds
Let the nothing storm in
Was it a sculpture or a recess

Vantablack was made for missiles
Or planes for defense purposes so dark
No eye could see it some voices are
Like that no one could hear them it
Is not good to be lost to be lost is
More than metaphor for spiritual
Condition I sit at the terrace overlooking
The green sea perhaps it is failure
That ought to be sought the voice
That fails falls silent Sheila's or
The body's the blue failed me the sun
Fails every evening I we you have all
Failed too everyone who strove all these
Long years for peace failed

When the sun goes down you move
Horizontal you become everything
In the world at once rather than waking
Like vertical where you obsess over
Ascend or descend or whatever rain
At the edge of the building spit forth
By gargoyles does drown yourself in the jizz
Of the world no shape of narrative
I'm lost but thrilled sun yellow still
Inside my self I am a pocket for the other
Day already gone Sheila hillbilly
Iconoclast seizes the song in the cage
Of her throat drawls not the edge of it
But its music entire

Sheila Chandra has been rendered mute
The ambassador of sound gray clouds
Compromise the day auctioned off
Siphoned off betrayed by the failure
Of nerves endings and science no cure
For Burning Mouth Syndrome she sang
In Uzbek contorted her tongue around
Words she never knew learned even
The language of the drum away from
Melody there is only harmony in the
Outer districts of the city of sound ordinary
Spaces empty bandstand atonal landscape
Sea's surface in the morning before the day
Traffics its contours

In a world governed by storm and noise why
Then should a singer not fall silent though
By great suffering her mouth that orchestra
Hall aflame the drone her most minuscule
Movement still do the echoes resound
Even now can I discern them Anish Kapoor
Explores the place sight disappears rich
Dark that opens he makes shapes of them
Invites you to understand or learn where
The effort to understand fails Agnes
Martin her shapes of white absence both
What when the throat fails sounds out does
Sheila still listen to music what does it
Sound like

Can she still feel music in her body can she
Vocalize even without technology of the
Mouth tongue palate glottis vocal cords
What is a voice Anish Kapoor granted
Exclusive right to work with Vanta-
Black she now communicates through notes
And gesture Vantablack made for
Military purposes like sound also used
For torture all sounds to wake you vibrate
Your brain what emerges as an echo from
Music as torture children on the beach
Playing god is sound or art or science
Shit and sex the body's echo what mess
Is left in the big or the little death

Calligraphy is a meeting point
Between abstract and particular
By certain combinations of visual
Marks to make symbols Chandra
Lost her voice around the same
Time I found mine at midnight
We went to swim in the sea so
We could be in the dark and not
Know the bottom but the moon
Lit up the surface so silver so
Slammed and then the boy
With the fear of failure falling
Architecture voice God depths death
He *swam*

That night we swam the full moon
Civilized us federated us gave us
Our nationality we who were lost
I have now lost what little heritage
I did have returned to the rude
Rough world long vowels of
Morning evening birds scream
No soft blanket falling to cover
But a throttling a suffocation
Of dusk no silence when the self
Stills the absence of noise is itself
Torture I cannot sleep tongued loose
Drones move through a riff by
A singer without papers

August 9 Eleanna takes me out on
The water Miller exploding the form
Of the novel itself I see now how Nin
Wanted to move away from his vociferous
Singing of the world as material to try
To construct a music of the way
The mind works still fed by light on the
Water a mute noise of engines under
Water as the boat passes the light-
House and heads out for open sea
Remembering in Palestine crawling
Down the hill trying to catch a wifi
Signal from the settlement untapped
Improvisation of space

At the stone terrace the gardener lingers
Clipping hedges while I work
One of the men targeted by Mossad
After the Olympics was a poet killed
In the street his poems untranslated
All the artists and writers killed the open
Space of the sea yesterday Eleanna and I
Went too far out went almost all the way
To Marseille we saw the pink-gray sky
Of wildfire I accepted the waves I found
In the chapters of the Qur'an to sing my
Way through turbulence draw a way
Through the waves savage wildfire and
The villages evacuated

We woke to the smell of burning air
A little cool smell of charred refuse
Colors muted last night the moon
Came clear nearly blue eyes too
Painfully large rough on the eyes and
Impatient but I wanted to look so
Badly for the meteors the sea
Crashing against the rocks smoke
From the fire obscured the sky
In the morning we rowed across
The harbor and realized fear of height
And fear of depth is the same just one
You see and one
You don't

Oh in the hows of Sheila Chandra
Sigh lents dew knot rain
She la Chandh-Ra's voice that swells
Of sun I am won what word quells
The chords in the box the mouth
Throat third voice sought
Dew naut reign in rain my hands
Hand me the rein will you sing can
You swing your votes vox fox
In the *howza* I learned scripture
Stripped her in the roost roust
All the birds to the blue the Moon-Sun
Singer singes now the world sound
Some echo wind echo wing

Who can born then believe
Beleaguered besieged be seen
Leagues from where you started
Parted in league with my liege
Legions of sound sound sounder
Her then be leaved darkest black
And be unseen a voice tracks back
For frown fawn fawned founded
Fundament firmly this firmament
This fund of sound born when you are
I did not want to be found how
Can you say that how can you now
Know what foe no she sang out flow
She breathed be real eve and lo

PHOSPHORINE

.

W   H   A   T

I   F   I   W

O   N   D   E

R   E   D   H

A   U   L   I

N   G   O   R

H   A   U   N

T   E   D   .

T   O   H   A

V   E   T   H

E   C   O   U

R   A   G   E

T   O   D   I

G   S   O   D

E   E   P   .

BRIGHTBYTHEBEDSIDEOFLASTLINGERINGSOMEONE.

STARSINTHESKYARESEENINSHAPES

O N L Y

B E C A

U S E O

F T H E

P O S I

T I O N

O F T H

E V I E

W E R I

N T I M

E A N D

S P A C

E . T O

G E T H

E R I N

V A S T

N E S S

W   E   C   L

A   I   M   O

U   R   C   L

A   M   O   R.

W   R   O   U

G   H   T   S

A   C   R   E

D   S   C   R

U   M   Y   O

U   S   O   U

G   H   T   S

A   C   R   U

M   S   V   A

U   L   T   T

O   S   E   E

K   O   R   V

A   U   L   T

T   H   E   C

U   L   T   U

R   E   D   R

A   C   K   E

T   A   N   D

I   N   T   A

N   D   E   M

F   A   L   T

E   R   A   T

T   H   E   F

A   U   L   T

.   T   I   M

E   S   C   U

L   T   R   A

N   G   E   O

F   S   K   Y

M   Y   V   A

U   L   T   E

D   F   A   L

L   E   N   F

A   U   L   T.

O   R   I   V

E   R   I   T

H   A   S   B

E   E   N   S

O   M   E   L

O   N   G   T

I   M   E   S

E   R   E   I

E   N   D   E

A   V   O   R

E   D   T   H

Y   T   O   N

G   U   E   .

O   H   D   O

G   I   N   H

E   A   V   E

N   G   O   D

O   W   N   O

N   M   E   .

o

FROM

CRIB AND
CAGE

o

SONNE ET

Ark now under fair gibbous dark
Far not fair yet there stowed
To the planet by grave obit
Written in physic to fail
Spawn to stop upon so won sent
Copped to lawn in spring sonne
Sprung from the clink a trap
I rote got
A string that swears under trance
Light a slight sleight train's
Late no one not yet in noon could
Spot light we know there
Is snow space nowhere now anon
Would rear real unreel and rare

GOOD BOY

Poetry is love for the felt fact
SUSAN HOWE

Good boy for know enow I no
I-land disappear in the aft oh brave
Noh whorl in the riven hand scriven
A ridge down which waves ruff
Aves spindle in air spun the jour
Made from amber antler bone
Nohow swale apport no one star
To now credo bray veneer worn
Who had known his feres so swole
He felt the beld heads en tranced
Felt trun a trem bren trough he
Swink to sain he wont to awin that
Awn unsparing the vessel respawn
And sware to be cered be yourn
Oh good boy good boy

GLOME

Look look loke turn in re sub
I search re cherche this twist per
vert the exchange but trot out
the trot trot the loke to nock or doke
En nar the end then noa trothplight
Light shard don a shared slight soor
Shoor of rone that swoon this night
Ye frayne the path wich way after
Now daft adrift in the rift between
Riff and clef nef not able to guide
Gullible skiff clop the hoof unfound
Frog untouch yet round this world
Doth trop or dop that glim that spun
A clot of lines seem cyme seme won

SONNER

Waul fill forest trin nev aoul fleme
Far then fly ore an gowl fell traved
Beast then fret bae doan fret such
Caul to shirr drawn coul the braul
Along brae shewn a shewel who lurk
In the lirk his lewk mean to fain stound
Fade the sonne fadensonnen celadon
Dusk the dunch of sound owl settle
In the murk I thought to thunge
By sonde found my way alonge
To weir none ken I luff it's all
I know to do in such temper timor
Tamp it is lost not to know in lais
Rift remet in trin rime deme

MAJOR

In the hoar between door and woolf
Own this glime of glim a glamer of dark
In it outline owre in the drinn on his hands
And knees he yet bruits cispontine scrip
No nonny governed at noon expelled
By oar dour our dower oyer ardor
Spent skint splinted in form by tintern
Unformed along spinet tune spinto
Sing note unheard unhoard relanded
Transpontine on the trot of spinks awing
In this ex change ex stat ex comm
Ex hale and hale hollering hallion hail
The wodge code vades wadi rode wide
Pelled across oud in hand on riant eyre

MINOR

Spilt somer sedgeward my clef
How I scrabble then loken loken
Lagan adrift borne swift along seif
Split of soma my spent mouth slocken
To spy quinks in the eddy where fell
The spliff whar you at field or fall in inure
Sense all things settle why not kvell
In stead of clef your soma spurl
Speer the mesne question since
Mien may manufacture manacle
Manual manuscript manus
And this unspooling of spawl
Speel into the bedizened daven
Be dizzy be quink be daw be ravened

DROM

Drom soun unfound confound
Fount unravel to sant follow ful
Dromos down chavish echo lown
Spanned years in dromic rounds
Babul sunt become sauch roads
To cop to cruise a curse to linge
Cruse fasten me breath drought
Under the door dram dowsed
For fair drank the dromophobic
Perced by mean dour trace ment
Dromond spare forth now kellick
Dropt trou tropic clothic suent
Corv deep drap corbis to maund
Dromo manic I fair froe for fent

CHORD

Bowed clever clavier clavering the clou
Spencer trailt open chawn flown half
Awake nor spilt nord yet haywire bowk
The ear a spail rasp in ward wound in
Wake or rowen town riven reev rive
River from reef reefed in wind wound
Reefer over the plouten map unreadable
Now from blear morn every chit calt in
Cald and collared mourn more in coir
We'll stay against the dawnpour when
Sonne du son sound and white lumen
Shine to swear a sweer skairy oath
This troth vive on the string that scrapes
And and vapor bowned down river sings

CALM

Calm now kin that can now ken
Kente come to claim what cain
Camo cult that can well conn
Catamaran into swell that dam
Will canine curet clean this kiln
Kelt to bear on the back of kin
Claim now ken that cant not ken
Skint kinot wail through smoke
And kelt dirge that sweel agin
The kin sent equant qualm the crime
What killed the store star or stent
Shunt I canto pin a sutra pen
Sintered bloke or bint who spoke
Such stolon threading sunken soke

TROP

Trop I well troop woal well voile
Un toile viol etoile spawn saeta
Sought sots on spot the violent lot
Scraped in stripes I strip achlaut
Trap or tell these traps swell sweet
Bitter fellen fell too strop scrape
Cut while Streep as Clarissa streels
The screen one as on trips between
Wars the hours violalate while
Wild wight streek their veil vail
There drail struck in second sight
Or sixth saat in Sanskrit but seven
In Hindi also Saatch = truth trop
De truth caltropped cant try trip

PRAYS

All hum do all law awl praise do
Open the mouth as stage or staging
Area and air to pray violint eyre spin
Skey sled skyey pent would fain
Refeel the villeins at hand their
Hantle of hant swelling to haunt
What's left of villan via askant
Low laws legible slayings legislating
The man on the ground his cheek
Prest knee in his back skance
Breathe canch and hance drawn
To slope slow down his breath awl
Laws prays to hum then do all reave
Detrave canch unhanced brieve

○

TANPURA

○

JUNIPERO SERRA ARRIVES

Now a year like bone
On a coast named for the *khalifas*
We bring date seeds as tribute to Muslim ghosts
Not the ones we harvested but the ones that haunt our own breath
We bring grass that will spread like Christ
If the spirit will not bend the body can be made to break

We stitch new texts into the air and ground
What chance to sky
What garden left
Your tongue shall tie
Don't say mountain haunted by bone

Don't say body don't say home
I too chose to live past the arrival of blades
Into the bodies of my forebears directing
Them like rivers or stone given
Such vague directions by god or
Man dear memory of myself

Wanting to climb wanting to know to be
Taught what is there
Each time I am reinvented as another human
Too many times to see the way
Gold and green are not the lights meant to grow
Here in an Arabia far from home

In a Spain lost to inquisition
Swept away that golden Jewish
And Muslim age in wind and sun
All its sea words blue and mispronounced

From books that did not belong were miswritten
The mosque roofs grow moss

Rain shines down through the late May storm clouds
What lonely span of ocean I crossed having renounced
My family of questionable faith on that middle island to come
To the valley of the Kumeyaay on a shore we will oddly
Call *Khalifa* to obey the dismembered god who in pastures
Of invasive plants summons me once more to storm heaven

CRUMPLED UP

Debris crushed to flowers made
summer you will thought swam
shard have this ember
rendered member of the body whose
urge surged swerve and shine
ocean opens shone hours
ours to contrail pretends
to sketch a shape of a flower against
infinite information of the sky
data mined eternal I in formation of a
day to mind the steeple wore
steep war mined the memoir of shore
meme war fought on the internet
where however there are interments
fast parsing the rationing shore
endlessness warned between each
wounded party marked
intersects insects in sects descend
to spend the real their wings
beginning that season's gnawing groan
of sex summer leaves shirring you can
at these moments open your mouth
imagine the *San Francisco Chronicle*
May 15, 1974 crumpled up sent forth
first paper to read then discarded
released found by Lenka one of an
endless piece of information met
for a moment given to Philip recited
received resited reseeded recedes
given to Kazim passed through the city
the situation an ovation oration
oblation ablation show me what you

pray for and eat save now in this flesh
archive what ought not be lost maker
of most light tossed sun rise up from
Rodeo Beach leaf me be reft left all
those bunkers in the hills their doors
rusted shut by metal or paper or
human touch weather concrete metal
paper or flesh we mark time on this earth

PULSE

To the sharp report in the dark the season comes home

Long tongue sound between hand and arm between mouth and flesh

Hold this moment river still what if it was my life

To return after years to the same province of danger

An old town you know like the handle the bump stock the trigger

I want to return to the boat that bore me from the far shore decades ago

What I lived in those languages I forgot the places I left I want to return to

Were we seen were we spoken were all the wolves baying

Met at the edge of the bright darkness of rain

Time cannot fulfill its promise to splinter return or slow

Vow this wheel this we will this weal we even wean

We in the world would wolve a low vow foaled

Worn low at the hip to be a solid soldier who soiled his sold soul

For the chance to be the first to aim first to fire to fly

In the cross hairs I am heir to no oar to hold I am on both sides of the gun

Toll as sound or cost one that never ends and the other never returns

Any embrace is the first error in meanings slope

Wrought by thought that one could reach another touch his shape

Known in two genders like Orlando whose tongue newly woke

To pronounce any word for god or man means to enter violence's fold

No oath sworn to save no salvation no salve no valor no ovation no nation

PETER

Is it unthreaded without music I come
To silence of god as the ruin of belief
All the strings of the body resound
Its own orchestra of always opening

Outside the sparkling silk rope of river
Marked by time and wind
History records its milky account
Water and light are granular

We are multiple beings always impossible
To hold or bind by the since wild wind
By the first gold dawn denying I ever knew
This world barely holds me

Seen through water or seen through
Light on the rain or snow
Makes you more blind
Why am I bound

To not declare in public my griefs or rapture
The way a body opens in love or death
A peony wilting past summer
How can we live without animal urge

To be measured or known like that
Chill in the air to mark that twice yearly chore
Carrying the plants in or out so they can live
All while knowing how ill equipped I am to help things live

It's true I denied but I did not lie
The cock kept crowing
What I said was: I do not know Him
And it's true: I did not know Him

THE DARK BROTHER

I talk to God but the sky is empty
SYLVIA PLATH

For a moment unspelled I had faith in God
But the government of that province cannot
Pronounce my name

Thank god for that because now my prayer
Can be catastrophic, apocalyptic, unspoken by any other
Weird enough to make an orgasm

In the sun-struck mind
I'm struck
Stroked, signed

Remember it took a deaf man to compose
The "Ode to Joy" so the laziest supplicant
Could stitch hours from scraps

I am hour I am hungry
And how I do hunger
Ours and all in all too late

Numinous this number
All existence numbered to paint
Cell by cell its color conscripted

How much I wanted to lose myself
But you cannot disappear unless you know
And I do not know

The bees have become believers
I talk to the sky but god is empty
A thief steals into the house

And who He is no one can say because the dog is for some reason
Silent and so unaware of invasion I lie awake
In the night wishing it were easier to die

THE UNLIKELY EVENT OF

A WATER LANDING

Banana flower
Pepper tree
Last globe of wickless lamp
Where have the Jews of Malabar gone?

Of the ancient population of thousands,
it is said only fifty Jews remain in all of Kerala,
only seven of them in Cochin—

Seven to open the synagogue
Seven to light the lamps
To wonder perhaps not where have they all gone but: Why did we stay?

It falls to me to ask this, on a winter day,
drinking ginger lemonade against the gruesome heat
while patrolling the market in search of a *mezuzah*

I want that prayer roll because by it one's own house is marked
as a house of god: the notion appeals when one's major religious expression
is one of denial

Now this junglee boy with wild hair
Not knowing his scriptures
Having thrown off all strictures
Thinks that the body is a road to god
Disassembles the temple
Desecrates the demands of the dead

The glass sweats
Even the ice in it is somehow warm and salty
I wander the market as three years ago I wandered Jerusalem

Looking for my friend Sameer without knowing
he had stopped a policeman to ask for directions
to the bus station and so spent two hours in detention
while I wandered a street on the so-called "Seam" unmolested
Passing without intention as Jewish

How odd that I trod without knowing the same water road
that bore here across the sea the Jews of India

It's always trace elements that tell the history
A lonely synagogue
And who among the throngs I see threading their way
through the souk of Cochin are the seven Jews left in Kerala
And who is keeping count anyway
And how many really are there left now?

Tangled roots of the banyan tree
Oh epic Chinese fishing nets
Dear every saint who fled
Why must I only kneel down to pray in unknown places
I davened in Jerusalem
I confessed in Valencia
I smoked sacred tobacco in northern Manitoba
I recited *namaz* at the Far Mosque
I spoke in in tongues and let a snake bracelet my bones

What I learned from that dry flicker, that shiver on my skin
Was how difficult it is for a human to shed his coat and go
Into the world as a new thing

To cross the water and live

Not to huddle in a basement room with all your belongings
Not to tuck a secret book into your sleeve
But to live in the light

"Junglee" is the worst thing you could be called where I'm from
Someone who lives not in a house or town but in the wilderness

Why in all the old pictures are our mothers so stylishly dressed and
    coiffed in Western fashion, chins lifted, gazing right into the camera,
    maquillage impeccable
When now they go bare faced and cover their hair and arms

But I changed too
Heat makes you human
And fear

Disappearing into the kingdom of heaven is one tried
and true method of awakening to life but there are others

All the rules, all the legislation that governs travel, eating, marriage,
where do they leave us?

And though the Jews of India, 50,000 of them, mostly all left
to go again across the water (though wouldn't you think
they would cling harder to a home after leaving Sefared to come here,
after leaving the Levant, though it has been centuries or millennia
and some trauma does fade) (though no it doesn't, it codes itself
into the DNA apparently) but fifty years after they left, fifty years after
they abandoned one homeland for another, new villages bloom
like groundwater from stone and claim they too are Jews,
that they are descended from the tribe of Ephraim—

Taught themselves Hebrew and all the minute rituals and observances

What makes you realer in God's eyes, practice, blood, or belief?

Summon the minion that we might stand against the scattering

There are new Jews in India

But here in Kerala, in the town of Cochin, in the Mattancherry district,
in the neighborhood still called by locals Jew Town we follow Miriam,
who feels like the last woman on earth, through light filled chambers
of an empty synagogue and wonder at the space time makes

After the market we go to the old Portuguese palace
where Marco finds his family name painted on the ceiling
among the royal and noble crests

I've never found my family name in history,
my family name is the name of a place, common as water

Never do I discover the history of my family past a generation
or two or three, so many borders have we crossed,
leaving behind all of what is supposed to matter—
houses, neighbors, papers, all those who knew us,
knew the shape of our ambitions and breath

In countless cemeteries around the world lie the remains
of my family's dead, unattended, untended, just drifting
into the earth untold

I've sat at a Sabbath table in Jerusalem, lessons written
right onto the wall, lights turned off at sunset,
a second little sink near the doorway for ablution,
those small daily chores echoing down for thousands
on thousands of years, are small settlements on the shore
of what is vast and unspellable

What is a town named, what is a name for

What journey does one undertake without turning
to kiss the Qur'an after you have passed under it
and who tucks a prayer book into the sleeve of his shirt

Why such devotion to the text itself rather than memorizing
the words and singing them through one's own body

Roots of the tree, this language, these water-words
that drum through the synagogue, not Hebrew but Malayalam
or English spoken by Malayalam speakers, extra vowels added
to the end of every word

Language like rain on the roof

What perfect sibilance to use a language of rain
to recite the rituals of people who passed like water
through this land, saturating it but unnoticed evaporating
into the blue linen of air to travel into flower petals
or the vitreous part of the eye or the saliva of a buffalo
or the trickle of a snail

Light rain, hot rain of summer

Rain wet on the roof

Rain falling in a tin bucket, rain in the ponds of the field,
different sounds of rain to describe the different languages
of southern India, the rains of India are Jewish rains,
the sound of diaspora, the words disperse, the sound of return
drawing a people in

The synagogues of India are emptied out and yet
in a groundswell, just a tiny blossom or a spindly green shoot
splitting through a crevasse in the concrete,
what does not normally happen
in the history of the world: new Jews

In the unlikely event of a water landing
the flight attendant announces on a flight between Denver and Austin

Oh junglee
with your lust and love for forbidden things
Don't you too hide away what you care about most?
Don't shame and guilt govern you every time desire swells?
Are you too got in you a little bit of Jew?

Laced by blue threads of liquid stitched through all time
Wicked winter filled
The oil in the wickless lamp
The glass globes shiver
In the parched seared air
As Miriam passes
The tiniest breeze riffles
The curtain hanging over the doorway

This is why we live in the world

Nothing so catastrophic as a plane falling out of the sky will ever happen

Nowhere in the electronically networked world
could a body ever go completely off the radar and vanish without a trace

The Jews of India have gone across the water

Between Denver and Austin in the air once, I looked down
at the desert to the horizon, no water in sight

Blue and green absented themselves
and all I could think about were the life jackets
beneath each seat, the life boats secreted away
somewhere on this plane

About the plane that disappeared, perhaps into the Indian Ocean

The same one that lies between the Levant and the Malabar Coast

What I bow down to does not know me

Safety and ignorance aren't they the same

Water folds over the vessel the summer I was free to learn that prayer

Prayers from hidden books resound in the abandoned buildings

Who leaves across the water

What and who do you leave behind

How do the traces still sing

What vanishes beneath the waves or into the earth or into the air

What pools up again from beneath the surface

And in the colorful streets in the old city of Jerusalem
I see others who look like me and wonder
now found now home now among all the others
who look and eat and smell and pray like you
what of Sefared might you deep and unsaid yet long for

What of the places in the west and the north and the east remain inside you

Do you ever still sing to god in the tongue of rain

Do inside your mouth still resound those days of heat and water
Do inside your ears still echo those green and blue sutras of Malabar

QUIZ

Does the fact that I have a cousin whose name is also Kazim
        make me more or less real

Strange this woman beside me drawing half a sunset
        then flipping the page

o

Questions draw me to the unanswerable

Can you guess how music ends or what feels like
        this brief lull of warm January

Never capable of tune I can only sing note by note or else in a tuneless slide
        between the unexpected registers of voice

o

Stephen and I climbed up the mountain trail as far as it would go before
        coming to a string across the path saying "raptor mating season,
        do not pass"

Coming down we met a desperate woman, tired and sweating
        "How much further is it?" she begged to know

I asked, "To where?"
        "I don't know!" she wailed.

o

Answers create the unquestionable

Is the other Kazim a question or answer

What voice sunset orange sings

266

THE FIFTH PLANET

Come, early summer in the mountains, and come, strawberry moon,
and carry me softly in the silver canoe on wires to the summit,
where in that way of late night useless talk, the bright dark asks me,
"What is the thing you are most afraid of?" and I already know
which lie I will tell.

There were six of us huddled there in the cold, leaning on the rocks
lingering in the dark where I do not like to linger, looking up at the
sharp round pinnacle of light discussing what shapes we saw—rabbit,
man, goddess—but that brightness for me was haunted by no thing,
no shadow at all in the lumens.

What am I, what am I, I kept throwing out to the hustling silence.
No light comes from the moon, he's just got good positioning
and I suppose that's the answer, that's what I'm most afraid of,
that I'm a mirror, that I have no light of my own, that I hang in empty space
in faithful orbit around a god or father

neither of whom will never see me whole. I keep squinting to try to see Jupiter
which the newspaper said would be found near the moon but
it's nowhere, they must have lied. Or like god, there is too much
reflection, headsplitting and profane, scraping up every shadow,
too much light for anyone to see.

MULBERRY

Down near Mott Street I wonder what is the actual border
between Little Italy and Chinatown, and if it doesn't exist then
what about any map's delineation, the name of that mountain,
or this border line?

That one-hundred-degree New York summer sent me in memory
back across years and time zones and oceans. July. Ramallah.
I carry home watermelon and salty cheese and white mulberries
in a crate marked "Israel." What is Chinatown anyhow?

A place people who left home come to find spices and meats
familiar to their tongue, and one street runs down the middle
of it but its edges like the desert trees and flowers
of Palestine linger.

What would it mean to not know the endings of things the way
in Palestine during Ramadan one doesn't know what to eat
or not eat and I couldn't find enough food to assuage the void
that being far from home opens up.

Yet the perfume of the *qarub* lingers on the tongue and I sauntered
toward Houston, crossing over from a *where* into a *where*, feeling
it was real, I was there. Somewhere, I don't know *where* but I was there.
That summer, whether it was Little Italy or Chinatown, Palestine was real.

AGHA SHAHID ALI RECITES LORCA TO AN ORDERLY AT ST. VINCENT'S HOSPITAL

It's May and the long cold spring has begun to loosen its stranglehold,
not out of mercy but because finally it accepts we are hunched down in despair,
and inside the hallways of the hospital, the patient stumbles and Angel
appears suddenly to hold him. "Ahn-hell from *Ec-wah-duur*," he declaims
in gratitude since sound is his most intimate lover now.

As they promenade through the wing, the poet begins reciting
what little Lorca he knows, "Por el East River y el Bronx los muchachos
cantaban . . ." and when he can't remember the words, his bird-like savior
with coal-black hair picks up the line. Tender Angel doesn't mind being held
      onto,
clutched, not as orderly but spouse because *like love, the archers are blind.*

At night he cannot sleep, so he asks Angel to come to his room and read
from his book: another poet in New York, another dark brother who sang.
While he recites from memory, Angel turns pages and follows along in Spanish.
Those silver threads wove from poet's mouth to orderly's ear like the
looping *nastaliq* of galaxies because *in the sky there is nobody asleep.*

Turn blue, the color of the sky and Mary's coat and the blood that races
back to his heart, while he recites all night long as on the Night of Majesty
the angels whispered God's words into the Messenger's ears. Angel is transfixed
and no one is sure when he switches from English to Spanish because in the
      deep hours
all words are music, and outside the sky *turns orange, turns the color of love.*

Eighteen years later there is a snowfall in April and *America drowns itself*
in machinery and lament. The hospital has been demolished, like the poet
    long gone
but in the wind on the corner of 13th Street and 7th Avenue, the verses of
    Lorca
linger like a secret kiss, and somewhere, somewhere in this city or country
    or world
Angel whispers into another's ears, *Cubreme, cover me with a veil at dawn.*

ICARUS TURNS FIFTY

Crudité and crackers. That's how my own myth starts.
I'm slicing cucumbers when the phone rings with that ominous tone
of a call you are not expecting. *It's happened*, I think. *He's gone and I wasn't there.*

And then comes his voice, alive and unbothered, same as it was,
maybe a tiny bit more gravelly, "Behta?" and haven't I imagined this moment
a hundred and eight times before, once for each turn in that Minoan maze,
once for each feather individually affixed to my back.

Sometimes I am silent and wait for him to speak, sometimes I hang up,
sometimes I am angry, sometimes I start crying, but in none of them do I do
what I do now, which is respond—conversationally,
as if it hasn't been decades since the labyrinth—"Dad."

Oh, a lifetime since I entered the blue deep, since choking to the surface,
treading water and scanning the thudding horizon for whatever rescue
by bird or boat I thought would come that did not come.

Perhaps it is not surprising that I grew up ordinary, the son of a great genius,
a once-rash once-lad who dared everything to feel fire, to be exceptional,
to reach the sun, to see what fish flickered beneath the dark surface.

He begins in the middle of a sentence, like he always did, talking about the virus
and grocery delivery and what's happening with my cousin's youngest son
who has decided to drop out of college and become a DJ and just like that I feel

the vibration of his voice banishing the old story, denying all my anger and
    sadness
of the decades since I somehow swam through the night to distant rocks,
weeping through my salt-raw throat. And so what is there to say?
I ask him what he shopped for,

and he says they don't have Weetabix and he drinks almond milk now
and the life where I flew away from him and he let me go just winks out
and a new life starts unraveling in its place.

For us there's no epic end, no begging the king of the underworld
to return the lost son, no father casting himself grief-stricken into the sea.
For a moment, I think: he always did invent the most exquisite prisons.

Then I think: or is this what we can bear, is this the price we are willing
    to pay.
He asks me are the cucumbers organic, and I ask him if he knows they have
    vegan cheese now,
and he asks me did I get those delicious rice crackers or plain saltines.

AFTERNOON LECTURE

The sharp sounds of a steel-stringed guitar plucked

Quavers down the cool first Chinook of autumn

Green plectrum of the ficus tree in bladed shadow

Anyone sitting close could not but hear in the vibrating air how long
    I've been locked up in the days

These buildings built by settlers to imitate Hapsburg architecture
    of imperial Spain

I am that human who could be the precise citizen untethered

Only cupid now my waiter a little messy behind his black mask,
    his forearms and neck scribed in ink

Each painting on the wall of the just re-opened museum is an eye
    that looks into me or a tongue that tastes me

Who in the afternoon lies down in wonder and aims to illumine

The waiter takes my card and my presence is read and registered

It's a hot Santa Ana that blows through the arches now and scatters
    the season that waged a claim for me

To be held in light and sound in a world behind doors whose history
    will stalk or stop stock still

After all I am more than embroidery or kiln-filed celadon made kin
    with calligraphy

This is the lesson of the California Colorists

ORCA ORACLE

There are three different kinds of killer whales in the Pacific, genetically distinct. The resident whales live in large family structures close to the coast, the transient whales wander out into the ocean in much smaller groups, and far out, relatively recently discovered are larger populations of offshore whales.

There are 274 resident killer whales in the Pacific Northwest, 200 in the northern group and 74 in the southern group. The southern group is roughly gathered into 3 matrilineal pods.

In this case, both predator and prey are endangered. And what happens when the prey is also of commercial value. Who wins.

The plot of the fourth *Star Trek* film revolved around an apocalypse being caused by the extinction of the humpback whale. An alien probe has arrived to investigate why it no longer hears the communications of the whale song which somehow amplified into space. The ridiculously named George and Gracie are set free only to be hunted by whalers. The climactic battle of the film is not with Klingons or Khan but with a whaling ship.

Only the summer diets of the killer whales have been studied. The northern resident whales mostly occupy the shores of British Columbia, while the southern resident whales range from Washington down the California coast.

I moved to California from Ohio in 2019, not sure I would ever move back across the Continental Divide again. Humans are animals too but we do not often stop to think about where we want to range or what food we need to eat for our own survival. For the one, we just follow the money and for the other we follow our appetite, which is never deep within in our body but just on the surface of the tongue.

The Salish Sea and the Puget Sound yielded up results to the scientists: prey remains and fecal samples, to be able to understand how the killer whales were surviving, what it might be (coho salmon or chinook salmon) we were taking out of their mouths.

It turns out chum salmon were the second most common prey. I call my partner "Cham" (pronounced "chum") which is short for *chamcha*, the Urdu word for "spoon." It's normally an insult in Urdu, used to refer to someone who's a sidekick or a hanger-on, but we started calling each other by this name after reading *The Satanic Verses*, in which one of the characters' names is Chamchawalla, which he tries to shorten and anglicize as Chamcha. It's not meant to be complimentary in the novel either.

It's the chinook salmon that is the most common prey species for the whales, the chinook who swim from the sea up the river to mate. I moved up the river too, from New York City to Rhinebeck, which is where I met my chamcha. Chinooks who are named for the Chinookan Indigenous Peoples of the Pacific Northwest.

The Chinook Nation is still seeking federal recognition which had been granted under President Bill Clinton in the last days of his presidency but revoked by the Bush administration.

Even though *The Satanic Verses* came out in 1988, I did not read it until 2002, afraid of the book somehow, afraid of what I would feel about it. What I feel about it is that it is brilliant, strange, and provocative. I heard Rushdie on a radio call-in show describing it as an argument for secular humanism. I called in to the show to tell him that while I thought it was a remarkable exploration of faith and how and why we believe the things we believe, I did not agree with him that in the end calculus it argued for secular humanism.

I do not now remember his reply.

Chum salmon are so-called from the Chinook word *tzum* meaning "marked."

I am marked as different in my own family, first tried to evade, then tried to rise above, now I travel among them, marked but cheerful.

While Scotty tries to fabricate a plastic that would enable the construction of a tank for the many hundreds of tons of water required to transport George and Gracie through time back to Starfleet Headquarters, Uhura and Chekov are trying to steal a nuclear reactor from a submarine to power the warp engines of the stolen Klingon ship.

The science from science fiction shows is always a metaphor for social anxieties or political crises at the time: warp speed, transporter technology, artificial intelligence, virtual reality.

The scientists who were tracking the prey of the killer whales could tell you where the prey came from, what stocks of fish it descended from, what its makeup was.

The Chinook is a warm western wind. When I moved to California, I moved to a city on a mesa, between the ocean and the mountains, in the traditional land of the Kumeyaay people, whose territories spanned what is now the US-Mexico border.

Humans and animals don't know borders really. We drew them on the map. It is tempting to say they aren't "real" but if you go down to the border near the city where I live, you can see how water distribution and terrain reconstruction has created two vastly different ecosystems on either side of the slatted, barricaded fence.

Music drifts over from Tijuana, whose neighborhoods extend flush against the fence. Which extends outwards, hundreds of yards, into the sea.

Saladin Chamcha is enraged all the time but suppresses his rage. He slowly, during the course of the novel, begins transforming into a horned and hooved monster, a devil.

When the Chinook is more available—in the summer months—it is the preferred diet of the whales. In the other seasons, chum salmon, halibut, lingcod, and other fish become larger parts of the whales' diet.

Paul Crutzen coined the term "Anthropocene" at the beginning of the millennium to define an age of the planet where ecosystems were impacted primarily by human endeavor. In 2016, Donna Haraway started using the term "Chthulucene" to imply that whatever humans had wrought had now traveled quite beyond them. While she was definitely referencing the monstrous or demonic of Lovecraft's Cthulhu, her spelling hearkened rather back to the chthonic: that things were beyond mere control of the human. The "Anthropocene" was over. That human and non-human, including the planet itself, were now bound together inextricably.

One could learn not only about the whales' diets from studying their fecal matter but also learn how far from their natal rivers the salmon traveled.

Because the *Enterprise* crew has traveled so far into the past to find the whales, they make humorous mistakes in their misunderstandings of technology. Chekov's Russian accent gets him in trouble as a suspected spy. Scotty tries to fabricate the plastic by speaking to the computer. "Computer?" he asks brightly. Dr. McCoy hands him the mouse. Scotty holds it up like a microphone and in that same bright voice says, "Hello, computer!"

There is, of course, no answer.

Throughout my life I moved from place to place. The longest I've lived anywhere are the ten years I spent in Ohio from my mid-thirties to my mid-forties, and the whole time I was there I was traveling, living for months at a time in other places.

Home is a wandering for me, or at least it always had been, until I crossed the Continental Divide and arrived on the western shore.

So what if George and Gracie were borne through time to save the future—in the present, our present, they still went extinct. We lost them.

247 resident killer whales does not seem like that many killer whales.

It's not a food chain, it's a food web. The building of a dam in northern Canada impacted the water, the fish, beaver, moose, muskrat, trees, and so on. Water flows. That Chekov with his Russian accent is harassed, chased, and arrested by the police, while Uhura, a black woman, is left unmolested, feels now quaintly and horrifically outdated.

The "satanic" verses of the titles are the ones that Lucifer supposedly slipped into the Qur'an when no one was looking. So you wouldn't know whose words were god's and whose were not.

In the Chthulucene there's no scripture or road map for what happens next. How can we manage salmon populations to support the southern resident killer whales. What impact will that have on other predator species.

And we now have to figure out how to manage prey species populations for endangered apex predators.

In a family, some stay close to shore, some wander out and return and others head for open sea.

Perhaps the answers are written somewhere in the sacred laws of the past or in the dizzying regulations and legislation of the present or the sympoeisis between human and non-human. As the scientists studying the killer whales finally conclude, "Further research is needed."

Computer? Hello? Computer?

SAUDADE

                             All be it through stone tongue

do the dead through tune tempt a sembled speech yet I

would fain feign silence in the wake of any angelic order

to speak of my life which for me was shame and a house

full of ordinary citizens who when the wind does undress

a body to ash cannot be asked its meaning

                                     and anyhow I knew only

one tongue neither German nor Portuguese and in the streets

of Lisbon didn't I like in Tamil Nadu when I tried Hindi

and the cab driver refused to answer speak with a Brazilian

accent as in "sauw-dodgy" to describe that mood soaking

the music haunting those streets glittering like snakes

so smooth you could slip walking uphill

                   yet after when time unspins (or maybe everywhen

is a pool (pool in Hindi means Flower) yes flower that contains both sexes) and must be touched to be in the world so if words

spoken in this apartment in the night between me and a man

who I would in ordinary life find reprehensible (terrible politics

on the the refugee problem and the European Union's response)

turn heated not heat that way but in the way of me

                                                    running my hands

down his slim torso kissing him with real hunger yet oddly thinking

of all that I threw away when I was going through the old box

of my school things like the biology homework and Latin conjugations

while I kept the odd play, the fake soap operas, the fan fiction already

by then wanting to live in that other world, any world, one I'd invented

or one that existed already in the oh well anyhow

                                          what if the ordinary life

is better that this one in which I don't really ever learn

for example chardonnay gives me heartburn always yet I never stop

drinking it even one time I put some peaches in it to pretend

it was that white sangria like the kind we drank that night in Lisbon and everyone was earnestly talking about when that moment

of feeling our life mattering evaporates

                    and I had said OK sure

I am in Lisbon and do not speak the language and maybe just kissed

a man (handsome, bad politics) in the street outside the bar but

if you were dead—when you are dead—and your tongue is stone

in your mouth and you have to make a tune to be known on

the other side who is it you are trying to speak to what are you

trying to say or have you merely chosen a house to haunt for example

a bar in Lisbon or the street in front of it kissing a man and then

ghosting your friends to go home with him

                    and then since

that night spent your whole life avoiding him while still looking

at his beach selfies on social media because (biology homework,

his pelvis thrusting into you, caedo/cadere, your mouth on his skin,

that fado music fading, and why do the Kurds want to come

here anyhow) you couldn't and still can't stand him—

CATHEDRAL

I walk instead along the river, my cathedral
not of stone or god but water made.

A woman in the median is shouting into her phone,
her diatribe punctuated by that most French of words:

"Franchement, je n'y crois pas!" and
"Franchement, je savais que cela arriverait!"

The Louvre roofs rivet tight the short horizon.
A discarded fan in the gutter, broken, fluttering.

Who was I when I came here before.
What were all the reasons I found all this so beautiful and unspeakable.

SOLACE

In Winnipeg there is a gravestone marked with my name
in which lies a man whose silhouette I see
in the mirror every morning

In the earliest hours I give extra water to the tangelo tree
which cannot give fruit unless a lemon or mandarin is near

When no one is awake and no friend is near
I find myself disappearing and yet able to hear
sounds half a mile away

Bell's theorem teaches us you can really only have one of two
worlds: a real world in which particles remain entangled even
at great distance or a local world in which nothing is real
unless it is observed

In either world I do not exist
June comes around and the lemon and the mandarin blossom
but the tangelo does not

Newton was as confused by gravitational action
at a distance as we are by quantum action at a distance

Einstein solved it by showing how the fabric of space bends
around large—planetary, lunar, stellar—mass

Local reality does not apply to the Universe

High above the earth still orbits the Micius satellite beaming photons
to the Earth in a continuing effort to understand why particles
are entangled across space and time

I have already outlived the man with my name by two years

We try pollinating the tangelo by hand but so far
there is neither bud nor blossom

Since the sun interferes with its mechanisms,
Micius only operates at night

The local world is not reasonable

There is no solace in the Universe

SYRINX, OR THE KISS

Reeds each gathered from the riverbank, pulped and pressed and
    inscribed upon

Do these forms have a future tense in the history of the year of
    diminishment, when the virus swept through us and claimed
    our breath

The year Sapphic fragments assembled in a string of code were sent in a
    flash across suboceanic wire from Mykonos to Manhattan

Each in our box we reach by voice broken down into data, transmitted
    not by radio wave or fiber optic but in binary code approximated

You may think of it as cold distance but it is why I, in 2021, in the
    mountains of California can listen to the throaty tones of
    Shreela Ray reading poems onto a tape in the Library of
    Congress, in 1979, her throat and lungs already itching with
    the illness that would eventually undo her

Shreela coughs, and laughs, her breath fills this room

As Syrinx was cut and bound by Pan to make music so at least this one
    part of Shreela is still echoing in the world

Are we brought then into one another's presence then somehow by
    sound even if it is the smallest band of possible registers, other
    parts of the voice elided, lost as in the winds of time the fires of
    the library blazed

Though wind and water are never lost but like Syrinx only change their
    forms

You change your form too, from body to electronic imprint, a ghost sent
in code through wires and air

What lonely aerial pulls those programmed voices from air like spirits to
materialize in the room, mouths moving but sound muted, an
atavistic echo of the oracles in mountain caves breathing deep
the fumes that would send them outside themselves to speak
with that other voice

The Qur'an tells of three races of beings: humans made from clay, angels
from air, and djinn made from smokeless fire

Djinn and humans live as mortals in the earth and I always imagined
that the explanation for my own reckless impulses and
intensities were due to some part of an ancient lineage of djinn
in my family

We're all djinn now anyhow, read, converted, transformed, transmitted

Was there some other legendary god who might have governed such
distance between a person and those they loved or is this
loneliness fully new, no mythic preparation possible

Perhaps it would be Syrinx or Shreela, her voice still floating through the
room, that could claim this space in the pantheon

The solstice passes and Brett urges us to climb the trail and see the
waterfall as its flow is ebbing day by day, water converting itself
to air as the rain recedes and the temperature rises

While in the days, gathered each in our boxes like books, we converse
without interrupting, the art by which our voices are carried not
permitting tone to cross over a tone

How then, can we neither cut across one another's voices, finally an
        intimacy, nor join our voices in choral note, be born in sound, a
        person is, and sound borne across mountain ranges and plains,
        across the diminishing Oglala Aquifer, across the ocean bearing
        the name of a fallen continent, might all bring us one to the
        other to the others

Is there a body politic without bodies with one another, so close we
        could see the movement of hair, the gesture of an arm, know the
        way a human smells, of lavender or citrus or musk or sweat

A body of the church, body of thought, body of work

And how might one experience love, siblinghood, fear, grief, death,
        lust, sex

It feels as momentous to me as when god left the garden and we
        stumbled forth without being seen, both djinn and human
        unseen and in that absence finally able to know

Do we speak then by voice or body or some inseparability of breath as
        both and these codices bound in bone and flesh that we call
        bodies or books, who do they govern in that space between us
        rendered as both eros and death

Only scraps remain of the poems from the ancient library, how will our
        voices recite them or will the future silence us

This long year unspooled in silence and distance and I desperately
        reached in long spaces for any friend to speak

From the mountain lake the water spills, too cold to swim in, the sound
        of it rushing over rocks filtering through the trees, that was
        what it was like to see your message flicker onto the screen

I speak nearly all day now, my voice scratched and disappearing,
    sometimes softened behind a mask

I mask my true terror: at never being able to touch another, never know
    another person again

And how can we communicate old truths—profound grief, passing yet
    intense desire, confusion

I contort my face into Greek masks trying to be seen, to be known

Did you love me once? At all? You drove me around all day, as you were
    supposed to do, in your beat-up Corolla, sticky with kids' drinks,
    telling me about how you and your wife danced as each others'
    partner in the ballroom competitions

When you dropped me off at the train station you hugged me tight and
    for a moment I let you fit into me and I was your partner on
    the curb and you put your mouth on my mouth and then you
    entered me

I was transfixed, I allowed your need partially by surprise and partially
    by instinct but mostly because I wanted to

I felt your body quicken and we breathed together and maybe a
    minute passed but who can say because aren't these bodily
    moments—one person's arms around another, his tongue in
    another's mouth—outside of time

Later, sitting in the benches of the station, waiting for my train, I got
    a text from you: "you didn't mind the kiss?" and that's how I
    knew less time had passed than I thought, that you hadn't had
    long enough to tell that yes I wanted to kiss you back, that there
    hadn't been any smoke rising to let you know that my body was
    converting cell by cell into fire

In our boxes we reach for each other the only way we can and we stake
        everything on this gambit: that the spirit of our intentions is
        enough, that we can love each other fully across miles, that our
        griefs and lusts are real

I waited until I boarded before texting you back, "please come see me in
        the city this weekend," and then I leaned back in my seat as the
        train bore me north along the peninsula, the fog over the harbor
        burning off in the morning sun.

THE STILLNESS OF THE WORLD
BEFORE BAUDELAIRE IN BANGLA

after Lars Gustafsson

To be close enough
To that must-have-been world
Fallible as a saint
Your foot free of its sandal

Rests lightly against mine
To smell your sweat mixed
With the flowers around my neck
Wilting in the heat

Outside in the street
A funeral procession groans on
While in the tent the crowd applauds
A translation: Baudelaire into Bangla

My mouth tastes the air
Your tongue pronounces me
Sounds out the insides
Your sole a portal gently there

My infinity falters
Will this feeling
—skin on skin—
Evaporate into

Young men in orange chanting
Flowers on the body
In virtue and loss
We are marigold listening

PETRICHOR LECTURE

hant I on the after noun wan
rain pourn in this ember
San Diego hand over
the reeding in hand then
routes racing to say
what fortunate when
rain can say

petrichorous petrichorus
lector on petra pale
through rain in the desert
does earth petrel rain
prickling my skin in
the mourn trickle
december trails

year's end petral withdrawal
future's end read
in the haptic drift's
happening I'm umbral
on board fated to fade
in rain untravel untrammel
uncastled rook

or king rooks sing petrachoral
morning in Normal Heights
rain on the ground or in air
an air not raveling but in strands
or points noted railing wren
arrive rooks and wrens
bend air in coarse weave and

waves the earth enters air querent
through rain and swears petricore
petrikouros pretty and soar the air
clears and wavers the sun sayer
airs and wayers the cours coeur
corps chorus kouros kaur
quai queer core care

.

CITIZENSHIP

If it isn't where you enter but where you exit

Who doesn't try to grab and devour what one loves

That last piece of the jigsaw puzzle fitting in

A ghost is not one who cannot let go but one who we cannot let go of

Streets wet with asters and deletion

June dissuaded by gray

My citizenship card found

Now I am neither one thing nor another

YIELD

Why did you not answer when I sent the shrikes to strike
the pane of the sky, what did you hear
when I called out in the night?

I have another life now. We dug up the lawn
and cut back the roses to their roots,
planted instead fava beans, chard, a fig tree, three papayas.

These are things that would never grow in the northern shores:

the great Mexican sunflowers whose seeds the parrots eat,
all the family photographs in which I do not appear,
the one part of my name no one else can pronounce.

It is a kind of hell not knowing whether or not you heard me.
Did you hear me?

The planet continues its spin but I am impaled
on a thorn of silence.

In the city on the mesa between mountain and ocean
we spent days cutting back the lantana so the monarchs
no longer come. In their place we planted avocado trees,
a pomegranate, parsley, and corn.

What could god have said to you that I did not?

We do not break the soil but build on top.
We do not separate the crops but scatter the seeds.
We feed ourselves in every season.

Marco takes bags of beans to every neighbor as a gift
Only one gruffly refuses, saying, "We don't want any of that."
In the night the shrikes come to say what you could not.

In all the years of voiceless song, what have you heard?
On my own and far from my source I had to make a home.
We scattered the seeds. We made a home.

SUKUN

The world is wound

Around me wound

That blessing that approaches

Reproach that world that would

Wind wood wind wound

How thunder would sunder

The sound there sown there

Is shown shone sewn

To a one that wood

Remain remains still

Won in the world could

Will I one will I shunned

Son soon swoon sukun

○

FAITH
AND
SILENCE

○

I remember the churches in the Coptic quarter of Cairo—underneath the ground, a dark staircase to the side of an empty courtyard, nearly overlooked. The entire church existed in the dark under the streets of the quarter. In that ancient city of a thousand mosques, some faith stayed silent about itself.

In Luqman:27, the Qur'an tells us, "even if all the trees in the world were made into pens and all the oceans in it made into ink, with seven more oceans to multiply it, still the words of God would not come to end." It's what poets dream about—that the entire universe is never-ending revelation and everyone with their ear to the ground might luck into prophecy. Still, with all the countless men and women in the beginningless generations who have "heard" the words of God in the rain, the wind, the stones, or from angels, we haven't managed to still the storm in the world or in our hearts.

"The Qur'an mentions one hundred and four revelations but only four of them by name," my wise father told me once. The four? The Torah, the Qur'an, the Injeel—a text revealed to Jesus, but now believed by Muslims to be lost—and the Zubuur (psalms) of Dawud. And the other hundred books? "We don't know their names," my dad says. "So the Baghavad-Gita could be one?" I ask him. "It could be," he agrees. In this way he taught me respect for all traditions of the world, but also respect for mystery itself—the one hundred missing books equal the one hundred names of god. And "one hundred" is itself perhaps only a metaphor for all the trees and oceans of the world?

For me, how you talk to God is paramount. I first learned to pray in another language I didn't understand. I was taught syllables first by transliteration and then in the Arabic original. It was hard work getting my tongue wrapped around the Arabic vowels and consonants that do not exist in English. Like the consonant in the middle of my first name and the vowel at the beginning of my last name, expressions of faith were unpronounceable.

My favorite of the five daily prayers was the first because you prayed it early in the morning before dawn, usually before anyone was up, in the privacy of your own room. As far as prayers go, though you were reciting out loud, they were secret. My next favorites were the noon and afternoon prayers because for some reason these prayers are supposed to be recited silently. Your lips move so people know you are in prayer but you make no sound.

For so many generations faith needed to be secret, under pain of torture or conversion. Silence is different than secrecy of course, but like the one hundred and four books, we cannot know the truth of our faith. And if we can, then there's no "faith" to it; such faith has all the charm of reading a dictionary. Because I couldn't speak to God properly—I learned to speak to God by rote—I drifted away from prayer as an idea of speaking to God ritually and toward different forms of worship: meditation, yoga practice, and a perhaps odd habit of talking to God or an empty room the way you might talk to your friend at the coffee shop.

A drone in music often accompanies yogic chanting or meditation. It's a single note held and maintained. Oftentimes if you listen carefully to it you can hear the harmonic sounds under the note—you can hear infinity in the singularity, as in David Lang's *The Passing Measures* or Sheila Chandra's *ABoneCroneDrone* series. The sound is supposed to organize or focus the practitioner on the inner sound—called *nada* in Sanskrit. I always liked that this same word means "nothing" in Spanish because nada is nada—no thing at all in the heart of awareness.

Not to say that there aren't "things" but after all, then again, maybe there aren't. For some time I have been in love with the paintings of Agnes Martin. Not with the blankness of them at all, but with the human touch, with the coolness, the emptiness of mind that can approach a canvas and lightly touch it. Each small gesture, each motion on the surface seemed so silent and thus a capable and capacious vessel of human emotion and communication. I find her canvases deafening in their concurrent embrace and refusal of simplicity, their motion, their restraint. You only think there's nothing there, but there's something there, something solid and real. John Cage taught us that there is no silence—especially not these days of intense electromagnetic radiation blanketing the air—and there never was.

Besides, it seems like any time someone thinks they have heard God whispering to them through the silence, there's trouble in it for someone. I think it's why I began to be attracted to poetry that was quiet about what it believed. Jane Cooper's work, for example, is haunted by the fleeting nature of a human life against the immortal scale of not God or a Creator but rather Creation, as if for Cooper the maker is in the made. "To live to be a hundred / is nothing," she writes in "Winter Road." "The landscape is not human / I was meant to take nothing away."[1] Her poetry always acknowledges that there is something that cannot be said, questions about existence that will not or cannot be answered. Earlier she writes, "birch leaves // make a ground bass of silence / that never quite dies."[2]

Talking to God is always essentially talking to Someone Who isn't going to answer. And for many of us, it is talking in languages we do not understand. Most people pray looking at their own hands. The body perhaps being the soul's ultimate fetish object. The body is the mortal part, the case of existence that the soul can look to for proof it is "real," that the world is actual. And of course—the urge is at the root of religion—the body looks at the soul in wonder, desperate for proof that there is more than the world, that there is some form of immortality, that death of the body is not annihilation of the soul or self, whatever those two things are.

In the Siva Samhita, an ancient Yogic text, it is written, "As in innumerable cups of water, many reflections of the sun are seen, but the substance is the same; similarly individuals, like cups, are innumerable, but the vivifying spirit, like the sun, is one" (Siva Samhita 1:35). It's as if in human life as in poetry there is an electric current in the air that animates each individual body or poem that is entirely unique and beyond the fleshly or verbal confines of that individual construct. Or as Donald Revell expressed, you don't find poetry in poems.[3] Because every poem—every effort at putting the ineffable into language—is destined to fail.

If there are a hundred unmentioned books in the world, it stands to reason, my father thought, that all peoples of the world, in all various times, must have had revelatory texts—why would anyone be left out of salvation, he wondered? It's an ecumenical Islam that I adore in him. "All rivers go into the same ocean," my grandfather was fond of saying on the question of religious tolerance. I thought him extraordinarily wise to have thought of such an image; of course I later found that particular quote in both the poetry of the Sufi poet Hafez and the philosophical writings of Swami Vivekananda. Vivekananda may have read it in Hafez, and I hope my Muslim grandfather found it there in Vivekananda's Vedanta writings.

But it's a one-way conversation, the idea of prayer. You talk to God. God is silent. You read the silence. For some people the holy texts are God talking back. Some people know the texts so well they can quote any part they find relevant to any daily situation. There are divination methods using the text to discover answers to daily dilemmas. Does it strike you as odd, a way of putting words into God's mouth? So much depends on the belief then of absolute purity of transmission of those texts. The titular metaphor of Salman Rushdie's novel *The Satanic Verses* was an imagined situation of a corrupted holy text. Mayhem ensued in art as in life.

The trauma of a prayer is not merely that we are forced into such a desperate situation as having to beg for something, but in the ultimate lack of an answer. Should the prayer be fulfilled we take it as an answer and if the prayer is not fulfilled we try for the justification: that God had other plans. But how might a god "answer" the prayer of a parent of one sick child but not another? You would say, "It was in God's plan," in which case we have to admit no one "answered" any prayer, but that events unfold beyond their pale.

In any case the rhetoric of prayer leaves the supplicant in a poor position indeed—we are powerless creatures, on the outside of Divinity, with no concrete influence on it whatsoever. No wonder children and adults alike prefer stories of youngsters—with broomsticks and spidersuits, wardrobes with doors to other worlds, or horcruxes that can hold the mortal spirit—to the watery vestments of faith, whatever it is.

Only some poems talk about life, describe objects and experiences. Other poems dream of music, dance, and prayer—like the wisteria in Lisel Mueller's "Monet Refuses the Operation," sometimes you find a poem that "becomes the bridge it touches."[4] It's a brave supplicant that continues to speak in the face of silence.

Revell goes on to suggest that one does not find "poetry" in poems, but that a poem is what is left after "poetry" has passed through a place. There is some ineffable experience that we might try to write about or describe, but often the experience itself remains slightly beyond the ken, the way one must not look directly at the sun, the way one must not, in some traditions, speak the name of God. We are left with its trace, a footprint, a curtain swaying with the breeze of someone's passage.

But how could I be a poet, how could I pray at all, when there was something I wasn't telling anyone, even God? Isn't absolute silence the thing that won't answer, the one thing you can trust, that you can tell anything to? But I couldn't even do that much. Ultimately it was my unwillingness to speak about the one thing perhaps most important in the mortal and carnate universe—my body's desire—that torqued my language into poetry. I never knew how to say anything directly and so I had to hedge in a hundred different ways.

It's naïve to say this hedging in poetry did not carve a landscape in my ability to express anything or even my ability to think through things in my actual life. To me Islam was never about the absolutes or the adherence to one interpretation of it—indeed it splintered almost immediately upon delivery. The one verse that was repeated over and over again in the Qur'an that I loved the most was "Surely there are signs in this for those of you who would reflect." The fact that this verse is used rhetorically and poetically causes many to miss its actual practical application: active engagement in matters of faith.

But I'm not to be trusted. I can talk about faith and silence in poetry and metaphor a million times but the most intimate of my self's secrets—love and desire—remained utterly separated for so many years from the most intimate of my body's partners in the world: from the seed and soil it came from, from the places it was brothered to.

When I learned to talk to God or to Silence, the lack of response was key to my willingness to speak at all. If God was never going to respond to me I would have to figure out Heaven for myself—I would have to know not by book but by heart what I believed and where I was bound. The Qur'an with its constant repetition of mysterious stories with various small and large differences, followed by that ubiquitous repeated verse—"surely there are signs in this for those of you that reflect"—seemed to back me up.

When you sit in a darkened room, talking to no one, even headlights on the street a hundred feet away seem to be happening right next to you.

Some years ago I lost a manuscript of poetry. Forty original pages, handwritten, not copied, not typed up, not anything. What I could reconstruct I reconstructed from earlier drafts, from memory, from prayer, and sometimes from dream. When I lost my folder of poems, I received so many different forms of advice. Robin said that the loss itself would change my writing practice. Gray said that I should write to the silent place itself. Marco said even if I couldn't remember the poems' words, the experience of writing them had already changed me, was already in my body. So it would be possible to rewrite those poems just from memory. Even if the "poem," the trace-record of poetry as Revell says, was gone or utterly different, the "poetry" of it ought to survive, the undamaged part, the eternal part.

But the poems and the poetry of the experience both were ephemeral—one written on paper with ink in letters, the other so intangible we can't even talk about it. Better to hold the silence. The silence—held as if physical, but ironically about the absence of the physical body: the folder of poems is gone. Gray told me, "You have to write to the lost poems now," and so I began writing directly to the condition itself of "lostness." It had something to do with my own silence, even perhaps my shame at keeping silent, at wanting that silence to be beautiful.

Silence wrote back as poems. If it was possible for Silence to write back was it possible—actually possible—for me to speak?

Like many writers I kept a journal by my bedside, either for transcribing dreams roughly in the middle of the night or even for attempting automatic writing while in a half-waking or half-sleeping state, the state when one's inner consciousness is supposedly alert—when one could attempt extreme mental feats like learning a foreign language or memorizing sacred texts simply by hearing them recited. I heard from someone at some point that it was better to allow the dream-worlds to pass unapprehended. Could I damage the pure secrecy of them by trying to write a single version? Wasn't it better then to allow them to pass like a stream, allow those images, phrases, words, and poems to remain in my subconscious mind to be forever fertile, forever feeding me? Should there be things one never says, not even in the darkest places of the night?

I found myself in Cairo, summer of 2001, accompanying my father on a business trip. Together we visited the Ra's al-Hussain masjid. A place of secret origins, this masjid was said to be the burial place of the head of Imam Hussain, grandson of the Prophet. Well, mostly Shi'as believe that Hussain—all of him—is actually buried in Karbala, Iraq. Still we found ourselves there, flabbergasted by the intense devotion of the Cairenes—mostly Sunni—to this most Shi'a of saints. My father told us we had to pray there and that if we prayed for anything there it would be granted since it was a place of such intense devotion. What moved him the most were the Sunnis themselves building and preserving this place.

Whether or not anything holy had actually happened there or anything holy was actually buried there was beside the point for him. And for me, it was an actualization of my own sense of spiritual doubt being ultimately the most sacred thing. I found myself in the burial spot where the head of Hussain, severed from his body, was said to be. I knew that if I prayed for something it would become real.

But what could I pray for? To have my body's love and desires disappear, change? To have the courage to speak? When it mattered—when it really (strangely) mattered—there was nothing to pray for. Because to "pray" would mean to ask for an answer.

I did not want to "receive" an answer, because I wanted my own.

Is prayer panic or in the most perverse way an actual denial of faith? That if God loves you He would come and take away your hardship? And if your hardship is not lessened, what could that mean? How could I pray for something? Was it selfish? Beyond all that—heartbreakingly— I could not choose what I wanted.

My book of poems *The Far Mosque* was about—in its conceptual form—the changing of the direction of prayer by God from the "far" mosque in Jerusalem to the "near" mosque in Mecca. In the story, the Prophet is borne aloft from Mecca to Jerusalem and then up into Heaven to receive instruction. In response to the historical controversy about the actual location of the far mosque, Rumi said, "Solomon's mosque is not made of bricks and bars . . . the farthest mosque is the one inside you."

So it might not be so odd that there's always something you are whispering to God that no one else is supposed to hear. The holiest place—the place you can jump up into Heaven from—is inside you. There's not such a long way—modern South Asian history notwithstanding, as my wise grandfather instinctively knew—between apparently different religions. In most religions public expression of prayer is preferred and encouraged, but for me poetry and prayer—both ways of talking to God, I guess—depend on secrecy or at least secretiveness. As much as I have ever been public about my life, who I love, how I love him, I had always held it back as a secret from those who knew me the best, the most, the every way.

Whether you are keeping a secret or keeping your silence it comes out in everything you say, every poem you write. I always wanted to tell everything but knew there was a piece of it—not a piece of it, but the thing itself—that I could not tell. Were the poems I wrote after the loss of the folder practice for a speech I was afraid to give? Is the form of a "prayer" just practice for actually talking to God? After years of comfort with these questions—comfort with silence, comfort with secrecy, comfort with the gifts in poetry they offered me—I found myself at last wanting only to speak.

How I said it I will not yet tell. After all, every poem has a secret place in it where promises are made.

For so long I worshiped the silence, the quiet place in existence, of being unwilling, or unable, to speak, but more than that, exploring the beauty and mystery of doubt and unknowing. How much have I been irrevocably changed by this pressure, the way a landscape is sculpted by the glacier advancing across it, but also as the glacier retreats? Everything feels strange now—my writing in my journal, interacting with friends and colleagues I have known for years, interacting with my partner, Marco. I keep wondering, can they tell something has happened? How will poetry and prayer work for me now?

In the hadith it is said, "Paradise lies beneath the feet of your mother." It is a part of Islam I find very easy to believe. But the body and the soul might not agree on its meaning. I think there is a place in the "self" where the flesh of the body's temporal existence and the quotidian awareness of the mind and the placid awareness of the eternal (usually very quiet) soul do not meet. I think that God is the place you cannot go.

For months I wondered to myself, any time I had a moment alone, When will I be able to go back to my parents' house? When will I hear my mother's voice again? If paradise lies beneath the feet of my mother, how will I get there?

For a man to leap up into Heaven, he had to go from the near mosque to the far mosque to the "farthest mosque." And what did he hear there? He was sent from silence back to his home—told the direction of worship was what was closest to him. For years I worshipped silence. In a single afternoon, the direction for my prayers changed.

NOTES

1. Jane Cooper, *The Flashboat* (New York: W. W. Norton, 2000), 236.
2. Cooper, *The Flashboat*, 58.
3. For more on Revell's complex discussion, see his *Invisible Green: Selected Prose* (Richmond, CA: Omnidawn, 2005).
4. Lisel Mueller, *Alive Together: New and Selected Poems* (Baton Rouge: Louisiana State University Press, 1996), 186.

ACKNOWLEDGMENTS

The poems selected from previous books were originally published in:

The Far Mosque, Alice James Books, 2005

The Fortieth Day, BOA Editions, 2008

Bright Felon: Autobiography and Cities, Wesleyan University Press, 2009

Sky Ward, Wesleyan University Press, 2013

Silver Road: Essays, Maps, and Calligraphies, Tupelo Press, 2018

Inquisition, Wesleyan University Press, 2018

The Voice of Sheila Chandra, Alice James Books, 2020

Crib and Cage, Pank Books, 2022

The essay "Faith and Silence" appeared in *Orange Alert: Essays on Poetry, Art, and the Architecture of Silence*, University of Michigan Press, 2010

The new poems were published in the following journals:

American Poetry Review: "The Unlikely Event of a Water Landing," "Mulberry," "Afternoon Lecture," "Petrichor Lecture," "Saudade," and "Solace"

AWP Writers Chronicle: "Sukun"

BOAAT: "Junipero Serra Arrives"

Colorado Review: "Peter"

Creature Conserve: Writing at the Intersection of Art and Science: "Orca Oracle"

Essential Queer Voices in U.S. Poetry: "Icarus Turns Fifty," "Yield"

The Fiddlehead: "Golden Boy"

Georgia Review: "Syrinx"

Gettysburg Review: "Agha Shahid Ali Recites Lorca to the Orderly at St. Vincent's Hospital"

Gulf Coast: "The Fifth Planet"

Queer Check-Ins (Smithsonian Asian Pacific American Center and Kundiman): "Prayer for Chasm"

Tampa Review: "Exit Strategy"

Witness: "Pulse"

NOTES

It was hard to "select." Lo and behold, or more likely low and be whole: I perhaps have been writing the same poems all along, the way waves are at once noticed—and have impact—on their own, but are merely expressions of the ocean and forces deep within.

I'm interested in the question: Does one write "poems" or "poetry?" In what ways is the question ir/relevant? Relevant only to revenants? Is a selected poem just remnants? A poem can live many lives. Can a poet?

One thing I learned assembling these waves together again was about water: the earliest three books here were written along the Hudson; the fourth written in a city on a bay governed by fog and wonder; the fifth and sixth written by the Great Lakes; the seventh in the midst of snow and polar vortex; and the eighth by the Mediterranean shore. The new poems here were written on the West Coast with the sound and sun of the Pacific along with the rainy, foggy months it engenders in early summer.

In Arabic orthography only long single vowels exist as separate letters; short vowels are expressed by diacritical marks and diphthongs, with a combination of diacritic and long vowel-letter. The *sukun*—which word means "stillness" or "rest"—is a diacritical mark over a consonant indicating there is no vowel to pronounce.

I owe more than I can say to more people than I can name, so I will be brief instead. I can thank the editors who published these books in the first place: April Ossmann, Thom Ward, Suzanna Tamminen, Carey Salerno, Jeffrey Levine, and Jim Schley. To Suzanna and Jim twice, three times, and four times over. And to Gillian Conoley, who read this book and helped me shape it. Thank you always to Stephen Motika, great and devoted partner and teacher and guide in the project of Nightboat Books, another expression of my life in poetry. At the end, for tending to every garden, to Marco Wilkinson.

NOTES ON THE POEMS

Renunciation

Epigraph is from Emily Dickinson's letter to Thomas Higginson dated 7 June 1862 (Letter 265).

In the Agnes Martin Room

The Agnes Martin Room is at Dia:Beacon in Beacon, New York.

Travel

The italicized quote is a light adaptation of a quote by Georges Braque, from *Painters on Painting*, edited Eric Protter (Dover Editions, 2011).

Dear Rumi

The name *Shams* means "sun."

Maya or Maa'

In Sanskrit, *Maya* is a deeply complex philosophical concept from the Vedas, describing the nature of the phenomenal universe as illusory. Connections have been made between these ancient ideas and the newest developments in quantum entanglement. *Maa'* is an Arabic word for "water."

Rhyme

Kythe Heller described to me a reading at which Olga Broumas declared "All the words in the world rhyme." Challenged on the assertion during the Q&A period, Broumas began spontaneously reciting to demonstrate her thesis.

Ornithography

Near as I know, I invented this word, meant to described the patterns birds write in the sky.

Pip

To Dan Beachy-Quick, whose writings on Pip in both *Spell* (Ahsahta Press, 2004) and *A Whaler's Dictionary* (Milkweed Editions, 2008) resonated.

Flower Gate

When the Báb, founder of the Bahá'í faith, was about to be executed by firing squad, a boy Anees, who had scaled the fence, demanded to share his fate.

Abu Nuwas

The pseudonym of a seventh century CE half-Arab, half-Persian poet who is said to have been equally fond of God, wine, and handsome men. His sobriquet means "the Father of Locks," referring apparently to the long tousled curls that were his signature look.

John

John Street in lower Manhattan, where I lived for a brief time in September and October of 2000, abuts the World Trade Center plaza.

Letter to Zephyr from the Once-Boy Hyacinth

In the myth, Zephyr the Spring Wind and the god Apollo compete for the affections of Hyacinth, son of Clio, the Muse of History. Apollo wins and Zephyr, in a jealous rage, causes Hyacinth's death.

The Labors of Psyche

When Psyche shone a lamp over the features of Eros so she could see him, Eros was forced by his mother Aphrodite to abandon Psyche, who completed a series of twelve labors in order to win him back.

Text Cloud Anthology

Created from a text cloud of "frequently appearing words" which appeared on the website for a volume of my selected poems that appeared in India.

All One's Blue

From Agha Shahid Ali's poem "Barcelona Airport": "Behold   how to hide / One must—like God—spend all one's blue."

Apasmara Climbs to the Mountain Lake

Apasmara is the demon of ignorance upon whose back Shiva dances as the world burns. He cannot be killed, only suppressed.

Hesperine for David Berger

After initially lodging charges and suspending him from employment, Yale University ultimately declined to pursue criminal charges against Corey Menafee and reinstated him to his position. Menafee became active in the campaign to rename Calhoun College, where his action took place. The college is now called Grace Hopper College, after the computer scientist and mathematician. The shattered window was given to the Yale Art Museum where conservator Carol Snow made the decision to not restore the window but exhibit the shattered pieces. Mohammed Al-Khatib trained with Carl Lewis for both the 2016 and 2020 Olympics but because of the pandemic-induced delay did not compete.

The Voice of Sheila Chandra

Chandra's singing career was curtailed by her 2008 diagnosis of burning mouth syndrome, a neurological condition with no known cause or cure. Though Chandra has regained some use of her speaking voice she remains unable to sing or speak at length.

From *Crib and Cage*

These poems were written in March and April of 2020 in the early days of the pandemic, when residents of California were in quarantine. Thus fixed in place in a time that felt suspended, I reached down into language—English, Middle English and its branches Scots and Middle Scots, Middle French, and Middle Norse, as well as some French, Spanish, and Latin. These dictions mix with contemporary slang and nonce words. Speaking in language is speaking in *langues*.

Minor

Helen Keller's list of English words—"manufacture, manacle, manual"— deriving from the Latin *manus* was invoked by Christina Davis in her introduction to a reading by Susan Howe.

Crumpled Up

This poem was written as part of "The Gifts," a project by artists Lenka Clayton and Philip Andrew Lewis, where Clayton and Lewis gave found objects to various artists and writers and asked them to respond. The project can be seen at www.lenkaclayton.com/thegifts.

Agha Shahid Ali Recites Lorca to the Orderly at St. Vincent's Hospital

Grace Schulman recounted the story of Shahid reciting Lorca to a handsome orderly at St. Vincent's Hospital, where he stayed during treatment for cancer. The rest of the poem is my fanciful invention.

Afternoon Lecture

California Colorists was the name of an exhibition I saw at the San Diego Museum of Art, curated by Anita Feldman, which included work by Wayne Thiebaud, Roger Kuntz, David Park, Roland Petersen, Raimonds Staprans, and Paul Wonner.

Orca Oracle

Sources: "Endangered Predators and Endangered Prey: Seasonal Diet of Southern Resident Killer Whales," by M. Bradley Hanson, Candice K. Emmons, Michael J. Ford, Meredith Everett, Kim Parsons, Linda K. Park, Jennifer Hempelmann, Donald M. Van Doornik, Gregory S. Schorr, Jeffrey K. Jacobsen, Mark F. Sears, Maya S. Sears, John G. Sneva, Robin W. Baird, and Lynne Barre, in *PLOS ONE* (Open Access); and *Star Trek IV: The Voyage Home*, directed by Leonard Nimoy (Paramount Pictures, 1986).

ABOUT THE AUTHOR

After a career in public policy and organizing, Kazim Ali received an MFA in creative writing from New York University, combining a study of poetry and dance. He taught at various colleges and universities including Naropa University, Oberlin College, and Davidson College. A longtime faculty member of the Community of Writers, he is currently is a professor and chair of the Department of Literature at the University of California, San Diego. In addition to publishing numerous books of poetry, nonfiction, and fiction, Kazim has translated books by Marguerite Duras, Ananda Devi, and Sohrab Sepehri, and has edited several volumes, including books focusing on poets Jean Valentine, Agha Shahid Ali, Hoshang Merchant, and Shreela Ray. In 2004, he co-founded the small press Nightboat Books and served as its first publisher, and he continues to edit books with the press. Kazim received his yoga teaching certification from the Jivamukti Yoga School, and for many years he taught yoga and trained yoga teachers at Farashe Yoga in Ramallah, Palestine.